Cover Photo by Raphael, London, 1928

Paul Robeson

BEARER OF A CULTURE

1926 portrait

Paul Robeson

BEARER OF A CULTURE

THE PAUL ROBESON FOUNDATION
WITH THE NEW-YORK HISTORICAL SOCIETY

Copyright (c) 1998 by The Paul Robeson Foundation
First Printing
All Rights Reserved
Designed by Gilbert Fletcher, Fletcher Designs
Edited by Janet Hulstrand, Winged Words Editorial Services
Printed by The Printing House, Inc.

Library of Congress Cataloging-In-Publication Data

Robeson, The Foundation
        Paul Robeson: Bearer of A Culture

ISBN: 0-9666711-0-4

All photographs, unless otherwise designated,
are courtesy of Paul Robeson, Jr.

Catalog produced by Jericho Productions, Inc.
Executive Producers Paul Robeson, Jr. and Lawrence Jordan

Table of Contents

President's Message

On behalf of the Board of Directors and consultant staff, it is my honor and privilege to welcome you to the definitive exhibition of Paul Robeson's valiant and productive life commemorating the centennial of his birth. As co-sponsors with the New-York Historical Society, under the splendid leadership of Betsy Gotbaum, we are thrilled beyond measure to share with the public the many facets of Paul Robeson's career.

Evidence abounds about the strong values instilled by his beloved father, Rev. William Drew Robeson and the sterling virtues he inherited from his maternal forbears, resident in America since the late 17th century. This exhibition catalogue provides tantalizing glimpses of both the substance and the nuance of Paul Robeson's unique experience.

Some observers judged him by the color of his skin, others by the "context of their characterizations." They missed the fullness of the man. His life—from 1898 to this centennial celebration in 1998—effectively chronicles the major events in world history during this tumultuous century. In the struggle for "full Negro citizenship," he was a leader and participant, an advocate and an activist, never willing to accept an "inferior brand of freedom" either for himself or for any member of his race.

In celebrating the legacy of Paul Robeson, let us also salute the memory of Eslanda Goode Robeson, his extraordinary wife, who had the foresight to collect and save these artifacts and memorabilia for future generations. Finally, this treasure trove owes its first public presentation to the passion and commitment of Marilyn Robeson and Paul Robeson, Jr., whose dedication to preserving, cataloging and sharing this precious legacy with the public has made this exhibition possible. We thank them for "keeping on."

Paul Robeson's life requires no embellishment or embroidery—he personified excellence, epitomized courage and embodied determination. We ask you to enjoy this historical and pictorial tour.

Bon voyage!

William Pickens, III
President
The Paul Robeson Foundation

About Paul Robeson

Football All-American,
Rutgers, 1917

Born in 1898 the son of a slave, Paul Robeson's achievements are unparalleled. Perhaps the greatest scholar-athlete in U.S. college history, Robeson went on to become one of the most distinguished performing artists of his time. During a decade as the world's top concert artist, he helped to establish the Negro spiritual and multilingual folk songs as recognized art forms. A top radio and recording artist, he also became the first black man to star in non-stereotypical roles in feature films. Still remembered for his signature performance of "Ol' Man River" in *Show Boat* and for his definitive portrayal of Shakespeare's *Othello* on Broadway, Robeson was one of 33 individuals, and the only African-American, selected for special honors in 1972 as a charter member of The National Theater Hall of Fame.

Paul Robeson's character infused and informed the popular culture of the 1930s and 1940s. For these generations of Americans, Robeson was the personification of integrity and authority. A man of indomitable courage tempered by profound wisdom, Robeson's humanity transcended divisions of race, ethnicity, gender and class.

Looking beyond his own formidable accomplishments, Robeson fought for universal human rights. His life, distinguished by dual passions for the struggle against oppression and a quest for the "oneness of humankind," leaves a powerful legacy to the world.

The Paul Robeson Foundation

The Paul Robeson Foundation was established in 1996 as a not-for-profit tax exempt organization with a mission to preserve and extend Robeson's rich legacy of humanism, civil rights activism, and excellence in scholarship, athletics and the arts. The Foundation supports and encourages academic, cultural and social initiatives that promote his profound human values in the United States and abroad.

Recognizing that two decades after Paul Robeson's death millions of Americans have little or no knowledge of this singularly accomplished African-American, the Foundation is dedicated to bringing long-overdue attention to the life and work of this towering world citizen. Its current priority is the organization and support of a national and international Paul Robeson Centennial Celebration in 1998.

As the sole nonprofit entity authorized by the Paul Robeson Estate to bear his name, the Foundation will employ the vast resources of the Paul Robeson and Eslanda Robeson Collections to develop a variety of Centennial programs. These will include exhibitions, films, multimedia presentations, educational materials and scholarships.

In addition to its Centennial activities, the Foundation is interfacing with other national and international organizations to promote opportunities and excellence in academics, athletics and the arts for African-Americans.

Foundation Programs

A century after his birth, Paul Robeson is still helping to build bridges of understanding among diverse peoples. As part of the Centennial activities, the Paul Robeson Foundation has initiated several programs that will reflect Robeson's ideals and inform broad audiences about his legacy.

A **Robeson Fellows program** will award annual fellowships to two outstanding African-American graduate students seeking advanced degrees in the performing arts.

A **multimedia tribute** will tour nationally, beginning in 1999. This two-hour educational, cultural and entertainment event will feature live narration and performances by media personalities.

The dissemination of extensive and comprehensive **educational materials** on Paul Robeson in all media for persons of all ages will begin.

A **lecture series and national and international conferences** will be launched during 1998 to engage scholars, students and the general public in an exploration of Paul Robeson's life.

The creation of a comprehensive **Paul Robeson Audiovisual Archive** will make his films and recordings readily accessible to the public nationwide.

The Paul Robeson Foundation is supported by generous contributions from foundations, corporations and individuals.

Board of Directors

Basketball, Rutgers, 1919

The Exhibition

Paul Robeson: Bearer of a Culture, an exhibition of rare photographs, original documents, memorabilia and audiovisual materials illustrating Robeson's life, opened on April 1, 1998 at The New-York Historical Society. The extensive Robeson Collections are the primary resources for this definitive retrospective, in addition to materials on loan from private and institutional collections in the United States and abroad. Following a three-month New York showing, the exhibition will tour major national and international cultural institutions

Singing 1950

The New-York Historical Society

Why do museums present exhibitions? We tell ourselves that our foremost institutional purpose is to educate the public in some way, and we understand that exhibitions are powerful tools in accomplishing that goal. We are also compelled, both institutionally and individually, to show our audiences something new, something we assume they don't already know.

What we as museum professionals rarely think about, though, is the power of exhibitions to extend our reach and to do much more than educate. We seldom recognize the greater opportunity exhibitions provide to provoke, to inspire, and to change people's lives. It is this more profoundly significant effect that we must now seek to bring about.

Paul Robeson: Bearer of a Culture, is just such an exhibition. Begun simply as a biography expressed through extraordinary artifacts, the exhibition has transformed itself, through the sheer power of Paul Robeson's life story, into much more. Visitors who have come to see the exhibition, young and old, every color, every political persuasion, have been caught up in the monumental life of Paul Robeson, and the chronicle of his unceasing determination has changed them.

As we move into the next millennium, we will continue to seek models of inspiration and examples of lives well lived. The New-York Historical Society is pleased and privileged to have this opportunity to share the remarkable life of Paul Robeson, a man who continues to help us all find a better way.

Jack Rutland
Director of the Museum
The New-York Historical Society
Exhibition Co-Curator

Presenting Paul Robeson

The occasion of the Centennial of Paul Robeson's birth provides a welcome opportunity to examine and interpret the life of this remarkable man whose deeds helped to shape the often tumultuous times in which he lived. Robeson's compelling story is in many ways a chronicle of the cultural and social history of 20th-century America. His extraordinary talent and exceptional achievements, along with his outspoken advocacy of the poor and disenfranchised, propelled him into the international spotlight, winning him the admiration and affection of people around the world.

The daunting task of creating a visual biographical presentation of a man whose complex life defies simple approaches was made infinitely easier by the extensive personal collections of Paul Robeson and his wife, Eslanda Goode Robeson. Wide access to those collections and a wealth of intimate details and background information graciously provided by Paul Robeson, Jr. and the Robeson family were invaluable to this endeavor. The combined use of unique photographs, rare documents, letters, memorabilia and works of art found in those collections or generously loaned by private and public collectors are the essential components in this visual presentation of Paul Robeson. The sounds of his magnificent voice singing the Negro spirituals, multilingual folk songs and show tunes made famous by him can be heard by audiences throughout the exhibition. Images from some of Robeson's many films and special appearances, as well as his eloquent words on issues of great concern to him and to people around the world, are available through video and audio devices in the exhibition galleries.

Paul Robeson was indeed the bearer of a culture, a uniquely American culture consisting of America's original folk music, Negro spirituals, work songs and that then-new idiom—the American musical. He took our folk culture to people throughout the world, and when he began to learn the folk traditions of other nations he added their songs—in their original languages—to his repertoire, confirming his belief in "the oneness of humankind" through culture. He steadfastly believed that "...a nation is ultimately judged not by its might but by its culture."[1] To that end, the Paul Robeson whom we present here has done much to help us define our culture.

Julia Hotton
Exhibition Co-Curator

[1]*London News Chronicle* interview, May 30, 1935

Paul Robeson portrait by Sasha, London, 1925

BEARER OF A CULTURE

Paul Robeson and the Universality of Black Culture

*"In my music, my plays, my films,
I want to carry always this central idea—to be African."*
                                        Paul Robeson, 1934

by Paul Robeson Jr.

PAUL ROBESON, one of America's greatest concert singers and actors, was willing to risk all in resisting the melting-pot ideology and challenging the cultural foundations of American racism. In this regard, he represented the antithesis of U.S. Supreme Court Justice Clarence Thomas in black life. Unlike Thomas, who is a model of subservience to white authority, Robeson continued the tradition, exemplified by his predecessors, of the independent black leader who champions the interests of his own people.

Robeson's personification of the African-American cultural tradition derived from the same source that provided Rev. Martin Luther King Jr. with his moral and philosophical base—the religious culture of the black South with its core values of American slaves. This culture, forged in the crucible of the slave-ship hell and the chains of slavery, constructed an intricate and sophisticated communications web that united the myriad of African ethnic groups scattered over a vast territory. It was centered around the traditions common to all African ethnic groups—traditions which nourished the preservation of each group's culture and were enhanced in return by those cultures—and was never understood by most whites.

In this sense, the slave culture had a universality which transcended the ethnic and religious differences among the large, diverse, and constantly changing black population of the U.S. during the 19th century. That universalist tendency was reinforced both by the inclusion of the black freedmen's culture and the necessary absorption of modified aspects of American culture. And since the Bible was the only book slaves were legally permitted to read, the religious expression of the slaves' culture became interwoven with the Judeo-Christian tradition. The African-American Church emerged as the cultural focus of black life in America by combining both the Afrocentric and universalist sides of the slaves' culture, thus supporting those blacks who integrated into American society, as well as the black majority left behind, outside the melting pot. However, American culture has always refused to acknowledge the Afrocentric side of black culture and has insisted on restricting it to its universalist side. Those blacks who are admitted to American society are required to abandon their Afrocentrism by pretending that they are children of the melting pot.

Although they were separated by a generation, both Martin Luther King and Paul Robeson steadfastly refused to abandon *either* their Afrocentrism *or* their universalism despite the conflicting pressures and blandishments of

American culture on the one hand, and black separatism on the other.

Three years before Reverend King was born, Paul Robeson made his spectacular arrival on the American cultural scene during the Harlem Renaissance of the 1920s. Together with his pioneering accompanist-arranger, Lawrence Brown, he went on to become one of the world's greatest concert artists of the 20th century. Through his identification with the universality of the black cultural tradition, he was able to embrace the universal essence of the ancient European cultures.

Those roots in the African-American slave culture came from my grandfather, Rev. William Drew Robeson, a runaway plantation slave from North Carolina. He was pastor of the Witherspoon Street Presbyterian Church in Princeton, New Jersey in the 1890s, built the St. Luke African Methodist Episcopal Zion Church in Westfield, New Jersey in the decade prior to World War I, and then was pastor of the St. Thomas A.M.E. Zion Church in Somerville, New Jersey from 1910 until his death in 1918. It was he who taught Paul the nonviolent assertion of full human dignity in the face of anti-black discrimination and hatred. My father referred lovingly to this legacy in his 1958 autobiography *Here I Stand:*

Paul Robeson portrait by unknown photographer, London, 1932

The glory of my boyhood years was my father...I marvel that there was no hint of servility in his make-up...From him we learned, and never doubted it, that the Negro was in every way the equal of the white man...

...I heard my people singing...from choir loft and Sunday morning pews—and my soul was filled with their harmonies...I heard these songs in the very sermons of my father...The great, soaring

Carrying the ball on the end-around, Rutgers vs Naval Reserve, Ebbets Field, 1917

Paul Robeson's father, Rev.
William Drew Robeson
(c. 1910)

gospels we love are merely sermons that are sung…[1]

The cultural significance of Paul Robeson's artistry was not lost on the critics. The reviews of his first concert season in 1925-1926 referred explicitly and even reverently to this aspect of his singing. The music critic of the *New York Times* wrote "His Negro Spirituals…hold in them a world of religious experience; it is their cry from the depths, this universal humanism, that touches the heart…Sung by one man, they voiced the sorrow and hopes of a people."[2]

And in an article in *The New Republic* magazine, Elizabeth Shepley Sergeant wrote that Robeson was "a symbol…of the increasingly important place of the American Negro on the American stage" and added that she hoped that "Paul Robeson with his evangelical tradition and Lawrence Brown with his Florida verve are establishing a 'classic' Spiritual tradition that will long live in American music…Let us give thanks that we were not born too late to hear this Negro Chaliapin render the Spirituals reverently, with wildness and awe, like a trusting child of God."[3]

However, not all of the songs included in the programs of his earliest concerts were spirituals. Throughout his concert career, one of his favorite songs was "Water Boy," a black secular song written by the well-known white composer, Avery Robinson. Some years ago, I found an interesting reference to that song in my father's 1929 diary: "Of course, technique might help me grow… —but that might not make me a *greater* artist. 'Water Boy' is my best record—[made] when I was untrained."

Seventeen years later, in 1946, his intuitive affinity for the song was confirmed when he received a letter, accompanied by an African battle axe, from a member of an anthropological expedition to a remote village in southern Angola. Several records had been played on a portable gramophone for the assembled villagers, and one of the songs was my father's rendition of "Water Boy." As the song ended, the village chief rose, went to his hut, and brought back a ceremonial battle axe which he laid before the gramophone as a gift to "the great chief across the water."

One might wonder how Paul Robeson could speak to the heart of an African chief through a song written by a white composer, but my father was not surprised. By then his search for his African cultural heritage had led him to research the origins of "Water Boy." He discovered that Robinson had heard the song sung by a black Alabama chain gang in a particular county of Alabama where the culture of rural blacks had its origins in southern Angola.

In the years between the Harlem Renaissance and 1946, my father traveled far and wide in a determined quest for artistic and personal growth. Like many gifted African-American artists and intellectuals of the 1920s, he chose to escape the stifling cultural atmosphere created by the melting-pot ideology. Because he sensed the essential shallowness of American culture, he decided to establish his artistic career in the richer cultural soil of England and the European continent. He also understood that the white cultural "establishment" in America would never willingly allow him to transcend its crude black stereotypes.

In 1927 my father brought me and my mother to London, where he became a dominant figure in the popular culture for the next decade. It was in London, he said, that he "discovered Africa":

> There is the future of the Black man. From there will come his real contribution to the culture of the world…I am now working at Swahili, one of the Bantu tongues, and have consulted many sources on comparative Bantu sounds. I found them most subtle…In these African languages is the content of the Negro spirit—the same spirit that one finds in music and sculpture….As one of African descent, I feel this strange necessity to (spiritually at least) find my roots.[4]

During this same period, his travels across Europe on concert tours brought him into contact with many cultures in which he found reflections of his own. In 1936 he wrote the following comment, which I found in a page of notes he had inserted into a Russian edition of poetry written by the great poet Alexander Pushkin, whose great-grandfather, on his mother's side, was Abyssinian:

> It is interesting that Pushkin, the shaper of the Russian language, like Chaucer and Shakespeare rolled into one, was of African descent. So the Russian language as spoken today passed through the temperament of a man of African blood….Pushkin means more to me than any other poet.[5]

By this time, Paul Robeson had enriched his repertoire with songs created from the folk idiom by many famous European composers, including Bach, Moussorgsky, and Mozart. A year later, he had an extraordinary experience which linked Mozart to the culture of African antiquity. He found himself on location in Egypt, during the making of the film *Jericho*. Henry Wilcoxon, his costar in the film, took him on a visit to the Great Pyramid of Gizeh.

As their guide led them to the Pharaoh's chamber at the geometric center of the pyramid, they all noticed an unusual echo. Wilcoxon urged Paul to sing a chord, and when he complied, the echo sounded like it had come from a huge organ. When the reverberations finally died out, Paul, without hesitation, stepped to the exact center of the chamber and sang the aria "O' Isis and Osiris" from Mozart's opera *The Magic Flute*. The entire chamber vibrated sympathetically like an enormous natural high-fidelity speaker, producing an unforgettable sound of unbearably majestic beauty. The richness of the multicultural symbolism was also very moving—here an African-American singer had made a connection with ancient

Robeson's mother, Maria Louisa Bustill

Snapshot of Paul Robeson on the Rutgers College Campus, 1917

With Jose Ferrer as Iago in the Broadway *Othello*, 1943

Still from the film *The Emperor Jones*, 1933 (photograph by Jack Shalitt)

Africa through one of Europe's greatest composers, whose music had been inspired by the legend of the African prince and princess who had colonized ancient Egypt. A perfect circle.

The famed British historian, Arnold Toynbee, made note of Paul Robeson's linkage of African culture to ancient Western culture in his book *A Study of History*:

> A distinguished Negro American singer...came to realize that the primitive culture of his African ancestors...was spiritually akin to all the non-Western higher cultures, and to the pristine higher culture of the Western world itself, in virtue of its having preserved a spiritual integrity which a late Modern Western secularized culture had deliberately abandoned...Paul Robeson was putting his finger on the difference between an integrated and a disintegrated culture.[6]

Toynbee is referring to the "pristine higher" culture of Shakespeare and his predecessors, which was far superior to modern Western culture; moreover, unlike most white Americans, he recognizes that Paul Robeson symbolizes the Negro who happens to be an American, rather than the American who happens to be a Negro. He goes on to quote Robeson, who had written:

> I discovered that...African languages—thought to be primitive because monosyllabic—had exactly the same basic structure as Chinese. I found that Chinese poems which cannot be rendered in English would translate perfectly into African. I found that the African way of thinking in symbols was also the way of the great Chinese thinkers...I found that I, who lacked feeling for the English

language later than Shakespeare, met Pushkin, Dostoyevsky, Tolstoy, Lao-tze, and Confucius on common ground.

My father's comment that he "lacked feeling for the English language later than Shakespeare" registers his affinity for Shakespeare's multiculturalism—a view that he shared with me a decade later when I asked him about Shakespeare's intent in the characterization of Othello. This universality derives from the ancient Anglo-Saxon culture of Chaucer, and it is my father's understanding of this culture that informed his definitive interpretation of Shakespeare's *Othello*.

In the Broadway Othello, 1943

Paul studied *Othello* in four foreign languages: French for its soft, almost caressing quality when Othello speaks about his love for Desdemona; German for a special kind of harshness when reference is made to military matters; Russian because of its extraordinary range of imagery and its capacity for the expression of subtle shadings of emotion; Yiddish for its light and sardonic humor and its bittersweet sadness. He also studied Elizabethan English and the pre-Elizabethan English in which Chaucer wrote, as well as the ancient Venetian and Moorish cultures in preparation for the role.

A leading British Shakespearean critic, John Dover Wilson, called the Robeson performance in the 1943-1944 Broadway production, with Jose Ferrer as Iago and Uta Hagen as Desdemona, the most notable one in the present century. It was also described, by Margaret Webster, the director of the production, in a 1971 radio interview. "Paul brought qualities with him which I never have seen equaled before or since," she said. "The moment he stepped on that stage, he was not only a black man but a great black man—a man of stature. Somehow or other, he put the play in focus."

Although she recognized the importance of bringing greatness to the role of *Othello*, the tell-tale words "somehow or other" reveal that she could not

Paul Robeson with (from left) Cab Calloway, Richard Wright, Fire Chief William Wesley and friend at the opening of *Native Son*, New York City, March 13, 1941 (photograph by Morgan Smith)

Paul Robeson at home in Enfield, CT, 1945 (photograph by Eslanda Robeson)

understand *how* Paul "put the play in focus." The reason for this becomes clear from an interview she gave to *New York Times* critic Elliot Norton prior to the Broadway opening of the play. According to Norton, Webster's idea of Othello:

> "...centers in the belief that both the text and the sense of the play require a Negro in the title part."...Everything points to his believing himself a member of a race which is not fully equal; it is this which makes him easy prey for Iago. Miss Webster points out that he is not sure of himself.[8]

Paul Robeson's approach to the role was markedly different.

> Othello has killed Desdemona. From savage passion? No. Othello came from a culture as great as that of ancient Venice. He came from an Africa of equal stature, and he felt he was betrayed—his honor was betrayed, and his human dignity was betrayed.[9]

My father believed that Othello's vulnerability to Iago stemmed from his feeling of *superiority* over the Venetians, a superiority which led him to pay little attention to what were, to him, their petty intrigues. This concept is based on a deep belief in multiculturalism, while Margaret Webster's view comes from the familiar assumption in dominant Western civilization that anyone from a non-Western culture *must* feel inferior.

The critics at the Broadway opening recognized the fidelity of Paul Robeson's Othello to Shakespeare's intent. Louis Kronenberger of *PM* wrote: "Robeson's Othello has so great a natural assurance as never to feel doubt; in a sense, he is lost once so utterly unfamiliar a thing as doubt enters his mind...Where shall we find an Othello to equal him?"[10] And, Howard Barnes of the *New York Herald Tribune* observed: "The magnificent Margaret Webster production is the first I have seen in which a Negro played a role obviously designed for him, and...it takes on more meaning and grandeur than I could have believed possible. There are those who have found Robeson's performance less than satisfactory, objecting to his deliberate delivery of lines in the early scenes, and his gestures of hapless anger as he is caught up in a web of jealousy. For my money, it is exactly these accents...which illuminate the tragedy for the first time on a stage."[11]

Margaret Marshall of *The Nation* was among the small minority who openly objected to the multiculturalism represented by a black Othello:

> Paul Robeson...performs passably well, but he creates no illusion...He is not the Moor as Shakespeare conceived him. Both Mr. Robeson and Miss Webster have tried to prove that Othello is a Negro; they have attempted also to prove that *Othello* is a play about race. Both theories are false and foolish...In Shakespeare's conception the essential

quality of the Moor is his foreignness. He is the exotic character—so exotic as to bewitch, for all his denials, the innocent English—or Venetian—Desdemona.[12]

During the play's pre-Broadway run, Leo Gaffney of the *Boston Daily Herald* had demonstrated his racial bias more crudely: "His Moor is too black, too burly, too obvious."

Rudolph Elie, Jr., the *Variety* critic, was prophetic in his review of Robeson's performance during the 1942 summer tryout of *Othello* when he concluded, "The play silences for all time the folderol centering around the furious controversy that Othello was not intended as a Negro and should consequently not be played by one. Fact of the matter is that Robeson's performance is of such a stature that no white man should ever dare to presume to play it again."[13]

However, Elie, like Margaret Webster, missed the main point—it was Paul Robeson's ability to tap the multiculturalism of pre-Renaissance Western culture, rather than *just* his color, that made his extraordinary performance possible. Salvini, a leading actor of Italian ancestry who was in touch with the ancient European culture, had also been an Othello far superior to the Othellos of many leading white *and* black actors who were imprisoned within the narrow confines of modern Western culture.

Paul Robeson's Othello made a powerful impression on an America in which the minstrel show was still a pervasive ritual, and some of the most persistent stereotypes of the black male were permanently undermined by his powerful interpretation at a time when he himself was only one generation removed from slavery. I can recall an evening in 1944 when a white man with a Southern drawl who was about my father's age respectfully asked my father for an autograph. *His* name was Robeson, he said, adding that we got *our* name from *his* father. Dad's face clouded over for a moment, but then he smiled, signed his autograph, and handed it to the man, saying: "Let's just say my father worked for your grandfather." After all, it was the grandson of the slave owner who had asked the son of the slave for an autograph!

The response of American popular culture to this challenge to its black stereotypes was to tout Paul Robeson as an *American* national hero, a living monument to that cornerstone of *American* civilization—the opportunity of an individual of humble origins, even a black individual, to reach the pinnacle of success. The clearest example of this can be found in the association of Paul Robeson with a staple of the popular culture: the musical *Show Boat* and its theme song, "Ol' Man River."

Jerome Kern, one of the greatest composers of the American musical theater, composed the music for *Show Boat* in 1926, and the famous lyricist, Oscar Hammerstein II, wrote the lyrics. "Ol' Man

With Uta Hagen as Desdemona in the Broadway *Othello*, 1943

Singing in Union Hall, 1944,
(Courtesy of The New York
Public Library, Schomburg
Center for Research in Black
Culture)

River" was dedicated to Paul Robeson; his rendition of it captivated audiences around the world, and it became his artistic signature. Edna Ferber, author of the book *Show Boat*, described a 1932 performance at New York's Casino Theater in a letter to the renowned writer and critic Alexander Woollcott:

> I...looked at the audience and the stage at the very moment when Paul Robeson came on to sing "Ol' Man River." In all my years of going to the theater...I never have seen an ovation like that given to any figure of the stage, the concert hall, or the opera...That audience stood up and howled. They applauded and shouted and stamped. Since then I have seen it exceeded but once, and that was when Robeson, a few minutes later, finished singing "Ol'Man River." The show stopped. He sang it again. The show stopped. They called him back again and again. Other actors came out and made motions and their lips moved, but the bravos of the audience drowned all other sounds.[14]

Listening to Robeson sing "Ol' Man River" became a landmark experience in American culture, so the lyrics, which changed over time, acquired a significant symbolism. My father had already modified the first two lines by 1932. Hammerstein had written:

Niggers all work on the Mississippi,
Niggers all work while the white folks play...

Robeson changed these lines to:

Colored folks work on the Mississippi,
Colored folks work while the white folks play...

The rest of the lyrics expressed a nondefiant lament, all that was allowed by the popular culture of the 1920s:

> ...Pullin' dem boats from the dawn till sunset,
> Gettin' no rest till the judgment day...
> ...Tote that barge and lift that bale,
> Ya gits a little drunk and ya lands in jail.
> I gits weary and sick of tryin'
> I'm tired of livin' and scared of dyin',
> And Ol' Man River, he just keeps rollin' along.

After his triumph in the Broadway *Othello*, Robeson rewrote the lyrics of "Ol' Man River" as a way of challenging the black stereotypes of the popular culture overtly. And his altered rendition of the song became the symbolic equivalent of the raised black fist, so it is not surprising that this version was not published, existing only as a *sung* version:

> There's an old man called the Mississippi,
> That's the old man I don't like to be.
> What does he care if the world's got troubles;
> What does he care if the land ain't free...
>
> Tote that barge and lift that bale;
> You show a little grit and you lands in jail.
> But I keeps laffin' instead of cryin',
> I must keep fightin' until I'm dyin',
> And Ol' Man River, he just keeps rollin' along.

Paul Robeson's refusal to accept the terms under which non-whites are integrated into American society was the reason behind his decision to challenge American racism head-on. Although *he* had been accepted as the equal of whites because of his extraordinary achievements, he rejected the basic framework of the society and demanded fundamental social, political, economic, and cultural change. He insisted that not just outstanding black individuals but the entire African-American people must be accepted as full citizens into all aspects of national life.

My father's rejection of the stereotypical images mandated for blacks by American culture coincided with his active participation in the civil rights movement of the late 1940s. In March of 1947, at a concert in Salt Lake City, he startled the audience after singing his final song by holding up his hand to still their ovation; then he announced that they had heard his last formal concert for two years, and that he would be singing songs of struggle to civil rights and labor audiences, rather than "pretty songs" on the commercial concert circuit. "From now on," he said, "I shall sing...only at gatherings where I can sing what I please."

He explained to the press that he had always refused to sing before segregated audiences in the South; instead, he sang at black universities where white people could attend and sit among their black neighbors. He added that he would continue to sing on college campuses and for trade union organizations after he left the concert stage.

Paul and Eslanda with dancer Paul Draper, New York, 1940

Paul Robeson with his son, Paul Jr. at a summer camp in Folkstone, England, 1938 (photograph by Eslanda Robeson)

Paul Robeson was true to his word, and his artistic appearances on behalf of civil rights and labor causes led him to become a spokesman for the growing national civil rights movement. On September 11, 1947, at a Madison Square Garden rally sponsored by the Progressive Citizens of America, Paul made reference to his universalist African-American cultural base in evoking a tradition which countered the ideology of the melting pot:

> Let us—a unified power of labor, liberals, Negroes, the Jewish people, descendants of foreign born, all oppressed groups...protect our true American tradition. Let us turn this country toward the course of history— a world of all the people,...a world where men of every race and creed may walk the earth in true dignity.

A year later, he spoke in a similar vein about his tour through the Deep South on behalf of the Progressive Party presidential campaign of former Vice President Henry Wallace. On that trip he and many others had risked their lives while leading the first voter registration drive among southern blacks since Reconstruction, and his words bear a striking similarity to those spoken by the civil rights campaigners of the 1960s:

> I've just come from a very long tour up and down the breadth of America...I was most moved by what happened in the Deep South. They told us...we couldn't come into Memphis, Tennessee....We went into Memphis. People said, "You're not going to have a meeting." We said, "We *are* going to have a meeting." And we got one of the biggest Negro auditoriums; a Negro minister gave us one of the finest places in Memphis.
>
> ...We went on to New Orleans; to Mobile, Alabama; to Charleston, South Carolina; to Savannah, Georgia...Here again, one felt

that....here for the first time it was not a question of...a few civil
rights—it was a question of striking at the liberation, the complete
liberation of the Negro people in our time.[15]

Fifty years ago, Paul Robeson was speaking of the "complete liberation" of
African-Americans, not merely "a few civil rights." Over forty years ago, he
rejected the limited absorption of all black individuals into the melting pot
which is still being offered today; what Robeson was insisting on was the inclusion of African-Americans into American society as a distinct people. I believe
it was this, and not primarily his left-wing radicalism, for which he was perse-
cuted so ferociously by the U.S. government for so many years. A decade later,
having survived the secret war waged against him by the FBI and the CIA, he
illuminated the path of the nascent civil rights movement of the late 1950s and
early 1960s. In his autobiography he wrote: "As I see it,...freedom can be
ours, here and now: the long-sought goal of full citizenship under the
Constitution is now within our reach. We have the power to achieve that
goal—what we ourselves do will be decisive..."[16]

At the same time, he believed that African-Americans had the potential to
become a decisive force in American politics if they forged alliances based on
mutual interest with organized labor, liberals and other minorities. In this context he saw no contradiction between complete dedication to the interest of
African-Americans as a people and close collaboration with white allies: "Even
as I grew to feel more Negro in spirit...I also came to feel a sense of oneness
with the white working people I came to know and love," he wrote.

This belief in the oneness of humankind...has existed within me side by
side with my deep attachment to the cause of my own race. Some people have seen a contradiction in this duality...I do not think, however,
that my sentiments are contradictory....I learned that there truly is a
kinship among us all, a basis for mutual respect and brotherly love.[17]

Paul Robeson was one of the main cultural links between the last generation
of black slaves and the generation of independent black leaders who spearheaded
the Civil Rights revolution of the 1960s. The creative manner in which he developed his cultural philosophy and used his artistic talents to further the cause of civil
rights led a panel of black historians to include Robeson among the ten most
important black men in American history. In an article published in the August
1972 issue of *Ebony*, they wrote that when his scholarship became better known,
Paul Robeson would "win recognition as the finest ideologist of black nationalism
since Sidney of the early 1840s...[and] as one of the century's most perceptive com-
mentators on the cultures of the East, the West and Africa." In 1977, on behalf of
a group of black notables who were protesting a Broadway play titled *Paul
Robeson* which they felt trivialized Robeson's life and misrepresented his character, the late James Baldwin alluded to Robeson's historic cultural stature and his
symbolic meaning to Baldwin's generation:

Robeson is not yet a historical figure, has not yet entered the limbo of
the public domain. He lives, overwhelmingly, in the hearts and minds
of the people whom he touched, the people for whom he was an exam-

ple, the people who gained from him the power to perceive and the courage to resist. It is not a sentimental question. He lived in our times, we lived in his . .[18]

Thus, it is not a matter of setting a historical record straight, or a matter of historical interpretation. It is a matter of bearing witness to that force which moved among us.

...The man the play presents is not Paul Robeson. That is all we are saying...We *must* say this so that our children's children's children will know better than we did how to honor and protect him when they meet him in their own lives.

It is my hope that the exhibition *Paul Robeson: Bearer of a Culture* will play a major role, not only in teaching the younger generations to "honor and protect" Paul Robeson but also in restoring and extending his powerful legacy. Then his light will be able to shine again in its full brightness to help illuminate our path into the twenty-first century.

1. Beacon Press, Boston

2. *New York Times*, April 20, 1925

3. "The Man with His Home in That Rock: Paul Robeson," *The New Republic*, March 3, 1926

4. From handwritten notes, 1934-1936

5. The book, the epic poem *Eugene Onegin*, and my father's inserted note are part of the Robeson Collections currently deposited at the Moorland-Spingarn Research Center at Howard University.

6. From *A Study of History*, by Arnold Toynbee, Oxford University Press, 1954, vol. 8, p. 501

7. From "Negroes, Don't Ape the Whites," *Daily Herald*, London, January 5, 1935

8. *New York Times*, August 16, 1942

9. Comments at concert, Mother A. M. E. Zion Church, Harlem, June 1958

10. The newspaper *PM*, October 20, 1943

11. *New York Herald Tribune*, October 31, 1943

12. *The Nation*, October 30, 1943

13. *Variety*, August 12, 1942

14. From *While Rome Burns*, by Alexander Woollcott, The Viking Press, N.Y., 1934, p. 126

15. From extemporaneous 1948 talk to Progressive Party activists

16. From *Here I Stand*, by Paul Robeson, Beacon Press, Boston, 1958, p. 74

17. *Ibid*. pp. 48-49

18. From an open letter by James Baldwin, 1977

Paul Robeson Recollects

Excerpts from the unpublished writings and transcripts of Paul Robeson from the Robeson Collections.

In 1922 Paul Robeson made his first trip abroad to star in the British production of a play he had acted in earlier in New York. Here he recollects this trip in a 1958 radio interview in London.

RATHER STRANGE, you know; as a young man, I never thought of being a singer or an actor. Somebody asked me about that on the train the other day coming down from Stratford to London. As a youth, my ambition was to be a lawyer. My father had a wonderful voice, and I thought of standing in the courts. And I studied at Columbia University in New York, one of the leading law universities, but I didn't stay in the law for very long. About the second year in college, I began acting in plays by some chance, and it helped me to get through law school, helped me to pay my way.

...But there's a very interesting story of mine that I came over [to England] way back in 1922. And not only came over, but had the privilege and great pleasure of playing a whole summer with Mrs. Patrick Campbell, which certainly seemed to me almost unbelievable. I had come out of school and played in a play called *Taboo* in New York. Mrs. Campbell had renamed it *Voodoo*. The playwright was a friend of Mrs. Campbell's, a Miss Wiborg from New York, and we opened finally in Liverpool.

I landed, I remember, at Southampton and went up to Blackpool. And I must say, Blackpool intrigued me. I never will forget—the waterfront was very beautiful to me. I used to go in and sit in the pubs and take a fruit drink every now and then. And then we went on from Blackpool to Liverpool, and an extraordinary thing happened.   In the play, which was about the Negro South and then going back to Africa, I was to be some kind of a chieftain. I fall asleep at the end of the first act—sort of in a dream I fall asleep, and I'm supposed to whistle; and before you know it I'm back in Africa. I tried my best, falling asleep, to whistle; and I still can't whistle, as you can hear me right now—I just can't whistle to this day.

And so I broke out into—"When Israel was in

Portrait by unidentified photographer. New York. 1926

Paul Robeson in car, with Eslanda and others; Oak Bluffs, Martha's Vineyard, 1927

Egypt's land; let my people go"– into a very beautiful spiritual that I remembered from childhood. As I sort of hummed this, I heard a voice from the wings: "Sing it louder; sing it; sing it louder." And if you've ever heard Mrs. Patrick Campbell with her whispers on stage, you'll understand why I began to sing this spiritual. And this was the first song I sang in Great Britain.

And then, to continue the story—I was quite startled when I finished my "Go Down Moses," I still heard this whisper from the wings: "Sing another; sing another." And so I really learned, I guess, one of my first lessons in acting: I got very sleepy again, I thought very naturally, and sang some others.

And it went even further. During the course of the play, when Mrs. Pat sort of lost a line and couldn't remember, she would turn to me and say with one of those beautiful gestures of hers: "There's now another song coming," as if it were part of the play. And when Miss Wiborg finally saw the play later in the week in Liverpool, the play had really turned into a musical. Luckily for me, I got very nice reviews from it and found out that I was a singer for the first time that I knew.

While Paul was in England, Eslanda stayed in New York, ostensibly so that she could keep working. (In fact she was undergoing recovery from a surgery that she had kept a secret from Paul, so that he wouldn't worry about her.) From England he wrote to her, telling her about his experiences—the excitement of it all, as well as the loneliness he felt without her there.

Week of July 24-31, 1922
Edinburgh, Scotland
Thursday

Darling Sweet,

We open here tonight in *Voodoo*. The audience here is a very fine one I understand— that is, high class. We hope to hit big. I shall have a final understanding also—you must come to me or I to you.

Miss Wiborg sent me your last two letters, the last one of which you wrote as you were on your way to the picnic. I know I'll have another soon. You must have some of my letters by now. I hope so.

So my little girl misses me so much? Darling, you must eat and sleep. I'll be with you soon. Sweet—what a day to look forward to. If it can only be when I go to Southampton to see my Dolly as she gets off the *Homeric* or *Mauretania*, etc. And she'll run to me and her sweet arms will slip around my neck and hold me tightly—so tightly; and she'll kiss me and kiss me, and I'll hug her and press her to me utterly oblivious of all save my little wife. How I want you, Sweet! How I need you to care for me, love me as only my wife, the woman I love, can....

Darling, our careers will be together. We will have our home first—careers next. My career will forever be less to me than my sweet little wife and family—Sweet, I love you so much I feel like "busting."

Will write my Dolly very often. Don't worry—you will see me soon. I need Sweet more than she needs me, if that is possible. Hate to stop talking to the sweetest girl ever—always and always your own affectionate and loving
　　Dubby ["darling hubby."]

Later on, Thursday, Edinburgh

Darling,

Just a little note. Am sending $100 by Miss Wiborg and have told her to give you any more you need. Suggested it would be about $200. If more, she'll give it to you. I'll put it aside from my salary and pay her back on her return. No chances on the money orders, etc. Too much to cable.

Eslanda Goode Robeson. Portrait by Helen Macgregor, London, 1928

Try to reach Plymouth the week of the 21st, say about Wednesday. The French liners stop here, so get one of those if you wish. Cable me at once to Shakespeare Theatre, Liverpool
—c/o Mrs. Patrick Campbell—of your plans.

Arrange at the hospital for a 2 months leave. Will not take any wild chances. Am not sure of our stay here.

We may not go into London until October 15; if so, can't tell how it's going there. If it fails, we want to be safe.... Don't be skimpy about money. I know you'll be judicious. Come comfortably and pay all things up, so you'll have no worry. I'll pay it back to Miss Wiborg. Get good 2nd class accommodations. Rates are lower, I understand, after August 15.

Be careful on the boats. Lots of "fresh guys"—watch your steward. Some women have a lot of trouble. Know you'll be able to take care of yourself. Waiting for you, darling—need you so much. Will be waiting for you when you come in. Lots of luck— nice trip.
　　Your own Dubby

Paul and Eslanda Robeson, 1930

Eslanda Robeson Recollects

Eslanda Goode Robeson was not only an intelligent, ambitious and effective manager of her husband's career. In addition to her crucial role in shaping it, she kept an eye on the future, and had a strong sense of his place in history. In 1930 she published Paul Robeson, Negro,[1] *an invaluable documentation of his early years as an artist. This excerpt from her book offers a lively view of New York in 1919, and of Paul Robeson's place in its cultural life.*

Chapter 5, GROPING: LAW, THEATRE, MUSIC

In 1919 Harlem had a complete life of its own. There were young and old Negro physicians and dentists, with much larger practices than they could comfortably look after themselves; Negroes owned beautiful houses and modern apartments; there were many fine churches; there were the Y.M.C.A. and the Y.W.C.A.; there were several chapters of inter-collegiate fraternities and sororities; there were Negro graduates from the finest white universities in America; there were Negroes in every conceivable profession, business, and trade.

About this time, immediately following his graduation from Rutgers, Paul Robeson came to New York to attend Columbia University Law School. He naturally settled in Harlem. Here he soon found himself among friends. Many children with whom he had grown up in New Jersey had come to New York to find work or to attend schools; many athletes with and against whom he had played while at Rutgers were now in New York; many people interested in athletics had read of his prowess on the gridiron and in other sports, and many had seen him in action. The Negroes especially knew all about him, and were very proud of the fine record he had made at Rutgers, both in scholarship and athletics. Paul Robeson was a hero: he fulfilled the ideal of nearly every class of Negro. Those who admired intellect pointed to his Phi Beta Kappa key; those who admired physical prowess talked about his remarkable athletic record. His simplicity and charm were captivating; . . . everyone was glad that he was taking up the dignified profession of the law. He soon became Harlem's special favorite, and is so still; everyone knew and admired and liked him; he was affectionately but respectfully known as "Paul" or "Robey." His unaffected friendliness, his natural tact, his great gift for "mixing," his real interest in everyone, soon made him "one of the boys." No matter how great his achievements then or later, his easy good-natured simplicity kept him from being regarded with awe; his many friends always felt that he was one of themselves who was doing great things, rather than that he was some far-removed celebrity. When Paul Robeson walks down Seventh Avenue he reminds one of his father walking down the main street of Somerville: it takes him

1 London: Victor Gollantz, 1930

Paul and Eslanda Robeson, snapshot, London, 1925

hours to negotiate the ten blocks from One hundred and Forty-Third Street to One Hundred and Thirty-Third Street; at every step of the way he is stopped by some acquaintance or friend who wants a few words with him. And always Paul has the time for those few words. In 1919 Paul strolled the "Avenue," and soon became one of its landmarks; he was often to be seen on the corner of One Hundred and Thirty-Fifth or One Hundred and Thirty-Seventh Street, the centre of a group. He could talk to anyone about anything. He had spent so much time with his father and in the Church that he had sympathy and understanding for the elderly, old-fashioned Negro. As a student himself, he had much in common with all other students; he could talk fascinatingly about games by the hour. He had a gorgeous bass voice, and could always be counted upon to carry the low part in harmonisations when "the fellows" got together at parties, or even on street corners, where they might be chatting and suddenly burst into song. He could always be counted upon to referee a game of basketball for the Parish House or the Y.M.C.A.; he could even be counted upon to coach a team or play on a team; he could be depended upon to sing bass in the church choir on Sunday mornings; he could "speak" or sing a solo or two at the local concerts to help fill out the programme. He was a member of two popular fraternities, one inter-collegiate and one professional; he was a welcome addition to any social gathering because he was a good dancer, a good "mixer," was liked by everyone, and could be depended upon to make himself pleasant to other guests. When Paul Robeson had been in New York one year he had become part and parcel of Harlem, and was affectionately regarded as her favorite and most beloved son....

At Columbia Law School Paul ran true to form. Among the white students were boys from Rutgers, Somerville, Westfield, Princeton; there were also boys he had met at other universities while on his many trips with the teams. Many of the student body knew him or knew of him. He was immediately commandeered to play on the Law School basketball and other teams. He made friends easily and soon became part of the campus life—so much a part of it that, when the graduating class of the university held its annual senior dinner at the Hotel Astor in 1920, he was a guest of honour at the speakers' table. R.L. Condon, the president of the class, who sat at Paul's right, said that "Robeson was invited by the whole class because he was one of Columbia's most brilliant men." Paul was as thoroughly comfortable at Columbia among his white class-mates as he was in Harlem among his Negro friends; he passed easily and naturally from one group to the other. He slipped into his niche in this world-known institution of learning and in this great Negro community with the same ease with which he had made himself an important part of the life at Rutgers, at high school, and in the towns in which he had grown up.

After he had won his degree in Law in 1923, Paul began to wonder what he would do. "Perhaps a political job to tide me over until I can build up a practice," he thought. But when politicians came to him with offers of city districts-attorneyship, or some other job, he found himself unable to accept it because of the many enforced allegiances it entailed. He must be loyal to the person who got him the job, he must be loyal to the party that kept him in the job; he was unable to fully approve of the person or the party, and so, felt that he could not accept a favour at their hands.... "I'll wait a little while," he thought, "something will turn up." And so he waited and something really did turn up.

A very successful and socially prominent lawyer who was a trustee of Rutgers invited Paul to come into the office of his firm to work. This was an

Marquee of Ambassadors
Theater, London, 1925

extremely important offer, because the firm handled big cases, and anyone working in the office could gain valuable experience in such work. The offer was doubly welcome to Paul, because it was almost impossible for a young Negro lawyer to acquire any experience in big legal work. This is easily understood when one remembers that there are no Negro railroads, few large Negro banks, few Negro millionaires with enormous estates to be managed—so there is no way for a Negro lawyer to get any practical working knowledge of big business unless he is taken into the office of a large white firm. This is almost never done, partly because such firms always have a long waiting list of applicants and have personal obligations to the sons of friends and business associates, and partly because of the great prejudice against Negroes. The few enormously rich Negroes and the large Negro insurance companies are loath to engage lawyers of their own race to look after their business affairs, because these lawyers have not had enough special experience to inspire confidence. And, since it is almost impossible for them to acquire such experience, the whole system forms a vicious circle....

Paul's opportunity was one of the rare exceptions, and he made the most of it. He spent all his time reading law in the office, and showed such interest in the work that his benefactor suggested that he draw up a brief on a phase of the famous Gould Will Case, which was then being handled by the firm. His brief was so thoroughly well prepared that his friend used it when the case was brought to trial. Paul enjoyed the work. But eventually the clerks and other members of the firm objected to the constant presence of so conspicuous a Negro in the office, and Paul felt forced to withdraw. His friend regretted the loss of what promised to be so valuable an assistant, and as they talked the mat-

Paul Robeson as "Joe" in the musical *Show Boat*, London, 1928

ter over frankly he realised how very difficult it would be for him to find another berth. He very generously suggested that Paul open an up-town branch of the office and take entire charge of it, but Paul felt he was not sufficiently experienced to undertake so great a responsibility. He returned to Harlem, uncertain as to what he should do next. "I'll wait a little," he thought again, "something will turn up."...

His usual good luck held, and again something did turn up. This time it was an invitation to play in Eugene O'Neill's *All God's Chillun Got Wings* and *The Emperor Jones* at the Provincetown Theatre. The Provincetown Players were really responsible for Paul's choice of the stage as a career. They form one of the most intelligent, sincere, and non-commercial of the artistic groups in America. The group is made up of some of the most interesting figures in the American Theatre.... Eugene O'Neill,...James Light, John Reed, Edna St. Vincent Millay, Theodore Dreiser...were some of its first members. The group was originated at a wharf in Provincetown, Masssachusetts, by a small number of people who wanted to write, produce, and act in their own plays....[It has] successfully established and maintained a stage where playwrights of sincere, poetic, literary and dramatic purpose can see their plays in action and superintend their productions without submitting to the commercial managers' interpretation of public taste.... The Provincetowners wrote and produced plays entirely for intellectual and artistic self-expression and experiment, and all the group fell to work to get the most good and the most fun out of each experiment...They naturally attracted people like themselves to their little group. It is small wonder that when Paul Robeson came to work with them he fell under their spell, and through them has remained under the spell of the theatre ever since. When he began rehearsals, during the spring of 1924, in the famous little theatre in Macdougal Street, his first friends were James Light, Eugene O'Neill, Eleanor Fitzgerald, and Harold "Gig" McGhee. At Jimmy's or Fitzy's or Gig's he had long talks with O'Neill about *Jones* and *Chillun*, about the meaning of the plays, about the purpose of the theatre. As he knew them better the talk drifted to the theatre in general, to life in general. They felt the existing commercial theatre, with its stock ways of presenting its unimaginative material, had nothing to give—except perhaps a superficial kind of entertainment. They felt a truly important and artistic theatre should not only present life but should interpret it, should help people know and understand each other, should introduce people to atmospheres, human beings, and emotions they had not known before, thus widening their intellectual, emotional, and spiritual experience and colouring their lives; should help people find more things of beauty in the world and in life. They were deeply interested in the modern expressionistic theatre of the Germans. "Why must a play be necessarily confined to three acts," protested

Gene, "when the life you are thinking about may happen in scenes, or in many long acts?" Gene broke away from the conventional rules of playwriting in many of his experiments. When he wrote *The Emperor Jones,* in eight powerful, staccato scenes, the Provincetowners enthusiastically produced it. It was much shorter than the usual play, lasting only one hour and a half in all. "Too short," said the commercial managers. When he wrote *Strange Interlude,* in nine long acts, the commercial managers protested that the public would never sit through a play lasting nearly five hours. "Too long," they said. Both these plays have achieved world-wide artistic and financial success.

Paul began to sense vaguely how great plays were written. When a sensitive, gifted artist like Gene went into a community, or witnessed a human experience, or felt the powerful influences of nature, he reacted emotionally to them; because of his great gift he could go back to the theatre, and, with characters, conversation, scenes, and acts recreate that community, or person, or feeling of the sea so successfully that he could make the people who saw his play know and understand and sympathise with that community, or person, or the sea as he did; and perhaps feel, according to their sensitivity, at least some of the emotional reactions he felt. This knowledge gave Paul an entirely new conception of the theatre. As spectator and as an actor it meant infinitely more to him. He could now get more from a play and give more to a play.

There were many long...fascinating talks. Gene had been nearly all over the world, had seen and done many interesting things; they all knew many interesting people—among them some of the great personalities of the present. Paul would listen eagerly for hours, for days, for weeks. Meantime they worked on the plays. Jimmy was vastly different from the usual director: he never told Paul what to do nor showed him how to do it. He never told him what to say; he merely sat quietly in the auditorium and let him feel his way; he often helped him, of course. When Paul had trouble with a speech Jimmy would sit down on a soap-box beside him on the empty stage, and they would analyse the speech thought by thought, word by word. "I think Gene means so and so," Jimmy would say, and they would argue and discuss. Very often Gene himself would come in to help them. Again Jimmy would call out, "Let yourself go, Paul. Don't hold yourself in; you look as though you're afraid to move." "I am," Paul would answer; "I'm so big I feel if I take a few steps, I'll be off this tiny stage." "Then just take two steps, but make them fit you. You must have complete freedom and control over your body and your voice, if you are to control your audience," explained Jimmy. They tore the lines to pieces and Paul built them up again for himself, working out his own natural movements and gestures with Jimmy's watchful help. "I can't tell you what to do," said Jimmy, "but I can help you find what's best for you." Paul was able to bring to both *Chillun* and *Jones* not only a thorough understanding of the script itself and its intent, given him by Gene and Jimmy, but also a further racial understanding of the characters. When he came at last to the performance, he never had to *remember* anything; he went freely and boldly ahead, secure in the knowledge that he knew and understood the character he was portraying. So that, at the age of twenty-six and very inexperienced, he was immediately acclaimed by the leading dramatic critics in New York as one of America's finest actors.... Even more gratifying and encouraging than the generous praise of the critics was a note written by his friend on the fly-leaf of the book containing his plays:

PROVINCETOWN PLAYHOUSE PRODUCTION

of

ALL GOD'S CHILLUN GOT WINGS

A Play in Two Acts

BY EUGENE O'NEILL

Directed by James Light

Settings by Cleon Throckmorton

Scene 1

Jim Harris	William Davis
Ella Downey	Virginia Wilson
Shorty	George Finley
Joe	Malvin Myrek
Mickey	Jimmy Ward
Little Girls	Helen McClure, Alice Nelson, Evelyn Wynn

Remaining Scenes

Jim Harris	Paul Robeson
Mrs Harris, his mother	Lillian Greene
Hattie, his sister	Dora Cole
Ella Downey	Mary Blair
Shorty	John Taylor
Joe	Frank Wilson
Mickey	James Martin
Organ Grinder	James Meighan
Salvationists	Barbara Benedict, Hume Derr, Louis Barrington, Wm. Stahl

"In gratitude to Paul Robeson, in whose interpretation of Brutus Jones I have found the most complete satisfaction an author can get—that of seeing his creation born into flesh and blood; and in whose creation of Jim Harris in my *All God's Chillun Got Wings* I found not only complete fidelity to my intent under trying circumstances, but, beyond that, true understanding and racial integrity. Again with gratitude and friendship.
Eugene O'Neill, 1925.

...With his success in the plays, Paul's interest in the theatre grew. He loved the life and the spirit of the group in Macdougal Street. Their freedom of mind, their friendliness, their informality, their complete lack of any kind of routine or system or efficiency in its irritating sense, charmed him at first, and then appealed to him deeply. Their leisurely, lazy life suited his own temperament perfectly. Their lives seemed to be one long round of lunches or dinners or suppers in the little food shops in "The Village," where prices were very moderate and the food and wine or beer excellent, and where one could sit indefinitely and talk, and greet friends and talk some more—sometimes even the proprietor joining in the discussion; and innumerable parties in the theatre sitting-room, or in the studio or flat of one of "the crowd." Yet how they worked when anything was to be done. Gene would disappear completely while he was writing a play. When a play was to be put on, all hands galvanized into action; every member of the group would report personally, and perhaps bring friends to help do the work; everyone lent a hand wherever he or she could....No one was too important to run errands, and no one was too unimportant to give valuable suggestions. Sewing machines hummed, telephones rang, gay voices buzzed all day and evening for weeks in the theatre before an opening. Jimmy worked relentlessly whipping the play into shape; everyone reported promptly for rehearsals and worked seriously and eagerly. Then, after the successful opening, everyone would join in the inevitable party of celebration; the round of sociable meals, parties, and long, lazy talks about everything under the sun would begin again.

The life appealed to Paul tremendously. He could be happy doing this kind of work; it was serious, worthwhile, important work, and yet it was fun. Apparently he could act—everyone said he could—Jimmy, Gene, critics, audiences, and last, but most important, his precious instinct, which always guided him, told him that he was on the right road. He had to use every bit of his brain and his talents for the work, but the result was well worth the effort; it was thrilling and satisfying. Then, after the work was done, there was the leisurely, interesting life again and the fascinating people to talk and listen to. He formed many interesting and enduring friendships indirectly through his work, among them Carl Van Vechten, Heywood Broun, Glenway Westcott, Emma Goldman, Niles Spencer, Arthur Lee, Antonio Salemme, and others. Antonio Salemme wanted to do a figure of him. "But I couldn't pose for a sculptor," protested Paul, "I don't know how." Tony answered, amused, "Good Lord, you don't have to *pose*—all you have to do is just stand there, and the figure will just happen. You are a great person," he said simply; "you've got a beautiful body, a beautiful mind, and a beautiful soul." Humbly, "I'd love to see how much of you I can work into a bronze figure. Please let me try." They worked all summer on the life-sized figure. The hot days of June and July found Paul posing, nude, with his arms raised, and Tony, in cool khaki, hard at work in the studio. The studio overlooked the fresh green of Washington Square, and was large and bare and restful...Tony whiled away the long hours talking about art. The human form is beautiful; we talk about the mind, the soul, the spirit; we don't *know* about them. If they really exist, they exist in the body, they must have come down through the ages and will go on to eternity through the body; life itself is controlled by the body, is perpetuated by the body; the body is supremely important in the scheme of things. The body has harmony, rhythm, and infinite meaning; it should be worshiped." And, Tony would fall silent, occupied with his work and his thoughts. Paul would often sing as they worked, sometimes trying out this song or that, experimenting with various vocal effects, learning songs; sometimes just singing because the mood demanded song. Tony always worked better when Paul sang.

Perhaps in the middle of an afternoon neither Paul nor Tony felt like working. "Let's go up and see an exhibit," Tony would suggest, and they would climb on a bus together like two children—Tony with no hat at all, Paul with his tucked under the seat. Paul always remembered those afternoons in the cool quiet galleries. Pictures began to mean something to him. "Start looking at the picture here," said Tony, indicating a focal point, "then see how your eye travels along without a break; or start here and your eye travels this way. Look at those greens: the green dress, the green cloth, the green bowl, the green leaves —all very different shades, but harmonizing perfectly." Paul learned that a good picture had form and rhythm. "Now look at this Rembrandt and this Jan Steen; you actually *know* these people." And, Paul, eager and quick to learn, would reply: "Why, I *do* know this old Dutch woman; she is motherly and kind, she believes in her country, she is comfortably rich, everybody likes her—I like her myself. That fellow is boisterous and jolly and very hospitable and generous; he is good to his family and friends, and is warmhearted. I know him too; I can hear him sing a toast in a lusty voice as he treats the crowd to a drink." Tony nodded approvingly. "That's a purpose of art: it should help us see and know and understand each other; it should broaden our experience; it should connect up the ages, the present and the future. Do you realize that these two people were painted more than three hundred years ago, thousands of miles away from here, and yet we know them well?" After several hours of wandering about they would

return to the studio and to work. Sometimes Paul would take Tony off to a baseball game at the Polo Grounds, and then indeed they were like two children. They sat in the stands eating ice-cream cones and hot-dogs, Paul explaining all the fine points of the game, and remembering the tricks he had worked out when he was catcher for the varsity at Rutgers. The muscular "winding-up" of the pitcher's arm, the fine body-muscle control shown in the expert fielding, the figure of the batter as he stood poised to receive the ball, struck it, then raced for the base—all fascinated Tony. They would return to the studio rested and refreshed.

All day, as they worked, people would drop in at the studio and the talk would continue.

…Paul learned more by listening to their discussions than he could have from months of reading and study. Glenway Westcott came in from his rooms next door very happy over the favorable criticism of his first book, *The Apple of the Eye,* just published, and full of plans for his next book. "I'd love to go to live in France a year or two, to get away from the American scene, and write my book about Wisconsin." But he had no money; no one had any money. But the money came, he went to France, and he wrote the book. Vilhjalmur Stefanson, the intrepid Arctic explorer, came in frequently. He talked about the new part of the world he had helped to prove existed. "It's quite livable up there; the people are sturdy and kind and friendly; they never bathe and yet they have beautiful skins; they oil themselves as a protection against the bitter cold; their diet is of concentrated foods and includes a lot of fat to keep up their body temperature." Stef's talk drifted on, opening up a new world for Paul, a new conception of territory, people, and ways of living. Niles Spencer dropped in and talked about his painting. "I think I'll go up to Provincetown and work in my old hut there. Wish I could go to Bermuda or Spain or somewhere; feel I need a change of scene." He went off to Provincetown, and later to Bermuda, and still later to Spain.

Often many of them gathered in the studio in the evenings. The talk sometimes drifted round to the Negro and his problem. Paul was a revelation to these people. Here was a Negro who had achieved intellectual and physical honors in one of their finest universities, yet he had retained all his racial qualities. It was easy to talk to him because he had none of the race-sensitiveness which usually complicates such discussions; he was not on the offensive nor defensive; he talked intelligently, honestly, and unreservedly about his people, was not in the least sensitive, discussed their virtues and faults and the probable reasons for them; and talked about his hopes and disappointments as a Negro. He showed his friends as much of Harlem as he himself knew; he introduced them to his Negro friends, good, bad, and indifferent, for Paul's friends were drawn from all classes. He brought records of Bessie Smith and Ethel Waters, his favorite Negro singers, and played them on Tony's Victrola for the crowd. One evening he took them all up to the Lafayette Theatre in Harlem to hear the singers in person. He discussed with profound dignity and real concern the problems and progress of his race, and was frankly proud of his fine Negro blood and African descent. He talked eagerly of his own hopes and ambitions: "If I can, with my imagination, body, and voice, build up the great tragic figure of *Jones* which Gene has written, so that that figure becomes the basis of tragic importance for the audience—make him a *human* figure—then tear him down in the subsequent scenes for the audience as Gene has torn him down in the script; if the audience, moved by his degeneration, his struggles, his fate, by his emotions—a Negro's emotions—admire and then pity this Negro—they must know that he is human, that they are human, that we are all human beings together. If I can make them realise fully the pitiful struggle of Jim Harris and reduce them to tears for him at the end—weeping because a Negro has suffered—I will have done something to make them realise, even if only subconsciously and for a few moments, that Negroes are the same kind of people they themselves are, suffer as they suffer, weep as they weep; that all this arbitrary separation because of color is unimportant—that we are all human beings. If some day I can play *Othello* as Shakespeare wrote it, bring to the stage the nobility, sympathy, and understanding Shakespeare put into the play, I will make the audience know that he was not just a dark, foreign brute of three hundred years ago in far-off Venice who murdered a beautiful, innocent white girl, but that he was a fine, noble, tragic human figure ruined by the very human weakness of jealousy. And,

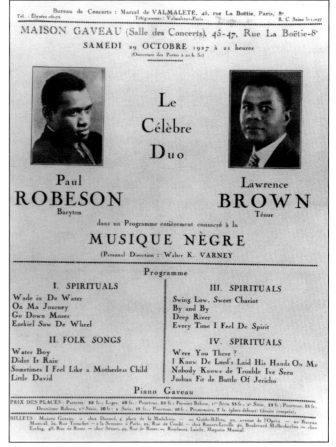

Flyer for Paris concert, 1927

with my music, if I can recreate for an audience the great sadness of the Negro slave in 'Sometimes I Feel Like a Motherless Child,' or if I make them know the strong, gallant convict of the chain-gang, make them feel his thirst, understand his naive boasting about his strength, feel the brave gaiety and sadness in 'Water Boy'; if I can explain to them the simple, divine faith of the Negro in 'Weepin' Mary'—then I shall increase their knowledge and understanding of my people. They will sense that we are moved by the same emotions, have the same beliefs, the same longings—that we are all human together. That will be something to work for, something worth doing." Paul talked on eagerly, finding himself, crystallizing his thoughts by giving them voice.

"I never knew anything definite about the sea except that it was cool in summer, great for swimming, and to be feared because one might drown in it—until I saw Gene's sea plays; then I began to really know something about the sea; to sense its power, its fascination, its romance, its beauty, its tragedy, its peace. Now, if I can teach my audiences who know almost nothing about the Negro, to know him through my songs and through my roles, as I have learned to know the sea without ever having been actually near it—then I will feel that I am an artist, and that I am using my art for myself, for my race, for the world." Then Paul would go over to the half-finished plaster figure of

Paul Robeson and Lawrence
Brown in Vienna, Austria at
Beethoven's grave, 1929
European tour

himself in the corner of the studio, stand up beside it, and sing, sometimes for
more than an hour. The little group scattered about the smoke-filled room on
the floor, divans, chairs, or against the walls would relax under the spell of his
great, soft voice, be thrilled by the almost barbaric rhythm, or moved unbearably by the stark simplicity of feeling in the songs. "I enjoy singing to you," he
would say simply, "You seem to get more than the voice, the music, the words;
you know what I'm thinking, what I mean, what I feel when I sing." Paul felt
the Negro had something definite to contribute to art, particularly to music and
the theatre: his quality of voice, his temperament, his vivid imagination, his
virility of spirit—all peculiarly racial. He hoped for the development of a definite Negro culture. "It would be splendid if Negroes would write books and
plays and music about themselves."

This group soon grew to love Paul and he them. They adored his easy
good-nature, his simplicity, his modesty; they admired his intelligence and his
great talents; they respected his dignity, and loved his singing soul. Today he
numbers many of them among his dearest friends. Before he knew it he had
slipped into his precious place among the Provincetowners, just as he had at
Columbia, in Harlem, at Rutgers, in his New Jersey towns; he was one of the
group, and was "Paul" to them all.

His step from the theatre into the concert hall was a natural one; his friends,
and even the critics who had reviewed his performances, had long admired and spoken enthusiastically about his beautiful voice. So when... someone suggested that
he give a concert of his Negro music in conjunction with Lawrence Brown, this sug-
gestion received immediate and important support from all his wide circle of
friends.

"We'll have the concert at our larger theatre, the Greenwich Village Theatre," said the Provincetowners. It was just the sort of thing they enjoyed doing. Paul was one of themselves, the concert was an artistic experiment, it was something about which they could be honestly enthusiastic. Fitzy arranged to let him have the theatre for the bare cost of operation; Jimmy and Gig arranged the stage and the lights to show him off to best advantage; Stella Hanau and Katherine Gay arranged for all the advertising, printing, circulars, mailing lists, posters. The entire concert was arranged on Provincetown credit. Carl Van Vechten, one of Paul's dearest friends, wrote many personal letters to the most influential of his friends advising them to hear this new and interesting singer. Heywood Broun, another very dear friend, printed the following article in his column, "It Seems To Me," in the *New York World* of April 18th, 1925, the morning before the concert: "I have heard Paul Robeson sing many times, and I want to recommend this concert to all those who like to hear spirituals. It seems to me that Robeson does a little better with such a song than anyone else I know; he is closer, I think, to the fundamental spirit of the music. Into the voice of Robeson there comes every atom of the passionate feeling which inspired the unknown composers of these melodies. If Lawrence Brown's arrangement of 'Joshua Fit de Battle ob Jericho' does not turn out to be one of the most exciting experiences in your life, write and tell me about it."

The distinguished Negro writer, Walter White, another of Paul's very dear friends, worked untiringly for the success of the concert. He talked to his many friends, both white and colored, and interested them all in Paul and in his work; he used the Associated Negro Press, to which he had free access, to broadcast the event from one end of the country to the other. Walter was one of those rare beings, a loyal and consistent friend; he often left his own very important work to take Paul down-town to meet people he thought would be interested in him. If he and Gladys, his beautiful wife, entertained guests of any special interest or importance, they always took care to include Paul. It was through Walter that Paul met Carl, Heywood, Konrad Bercovici, the Van Dorens, the Spingarns, and many other interesting and charming people.

Paul's friends in Harlem talked about the importance of a programme of all-Negro music. His Negro friends uptown and his white friends down-town joined hands and worked for the success of the concert. Together they created a great general interest in the event, and on that Sunday evening, April 19th, 1925, when the loyal and eager Provincetowners, dressed in evening clothes to do their friend honor, gathered in a body at the Greenwich Village Theatre, they were surprised and delighted to find a huge crowd filling the lobby and the sidewalk in front of the theatre, and to learn that all the seats and all the standing-room had been sold, and that they would have to stand in the wings to hear the concert. This they gladly did, and threw words of encouragement and friendly, reassuring jokes to Paul and Larry as they strode on to the stage, very nervous and frightened. The roar after roar of enthusiastic and anticipatory applause which greeted them from the audience so startled and disarmed them that they had finished their first group of songs before they remembered to be concerned about voice and piano; they had forgotten themselves in the excitement, and had sung their lovely music simply, unaffectedly, and beautifully. At the end of the programme the entire audience remained seated, clamoring for more; they gave many encores, and finally, tired out, could only bow and smile their appreciation to the still applauding audience. It was a memorable evening.

Singing in Albert Hall, London, 1929

The next day, many of the New York musical critics proclaimed Paul's voice one of great beauty and power, and his personality unique on the concert stage. The *World* declared that "all those who listened last night to the first concert in this country made up entirely of Negro music—if one may count out the chorals from Fiske and so forth— may have been present at a turning point, one of those thin points of time in which a star is born and not yet visible—the first appearance of this folk wealth to be made without deference or apology. Paul Robeson's voice is difficult to describe. It is a voice in which deep bells ring. It has all it needs—perfect pace, beautiful enunciation." The *Evening Post's* verdict was that "he gives to this characteristic music exactly the quality it has in the place of its origin."

Of his second concert, on May 3rd, 1925, the *Evening Post* wrote: "Last night Paul Robeson and Lawrence Brown gave their second concert of the season, and revealed once more their mastery of the songs of their people. They provided this reporter with a thrill as exquisite as the revelation of Chaliapin singing Moussourgsky. For Mr. Robeson combines with a glorious rich and mellow voice a dramatic restraint and power that seems to hold untold thunder behind each song. His spirituals, sung with classic simplicity, have a particular flavour of encompassing some universal tragedy of spirit within the bounds of the naive form of folk song. And, while Mr. Robeson offered the dramatic foundation of the recital, Mr. Brown's sympathetic singing and piano arrangements completed a concert that brought cheers from the Sunday night gathering."

An enterprising concert manager promptly signed Paul and Larry for an extensive concert tour for the following year.

Robeson's Writings on Culture

In the 1930s, Paul Robeson embarked on a determined and comprehensive quest for his cultural roots in Africa and their connections with the cultures of the East. The depth of his scholarship is revealed in these hand-written notes found among his personal papers.

Four excerpts are presented below: the first and last deal with Africa and the American Negro; the middle two explore "Nationalism" and "Materialism." The first excerpt is titled simply: "Negro problem— Negro in West [and] in Africa." (1934)

Now, at the other end of [the] world, we have [the] Chinese who have lived almost as artists concerned mainly with [the] inner development of *man*— concerned with this *psyche* which we have neglected, and with *man* in relation to his fellow man as a "*social*" *being*, not as a kind of "lone wolf." Naturally, many generations devoted to this have evolved a man with much deeper *capacity* for good life than our scientific man of West. Present-day philosophers see some combinations of the two points of view in the future. The West will carry scientific method Eastward and come back, as many times before in World History, with spiritual heritage of the East.

It is against this background that I see the African [as] the hope of the black man in the world of the future. This may seem a surprising statement. [But] I am firmly convinced that the Negro in the Western world—in North America, South America, the West Indies, the Caribbean—has become Western for good or evil, and will contribute to the culture of his respective social milieu. That is, the American Negro will contribute, as he has in the past, to American culture. In fact, he may do most of the contributing.

But after all, Africa is the black man's home, and the pure expression must come from there. In fact, the only hope for a future Negro expression among Western Negroes rests upon this pure *source* in Africa. Otherwise, foreign elements will completely destroy the Negro element in the *West*. This latter seems at present probable, but there is still an outside chance that the black man in the West will look back to the source for inspiration; but this can only be if Africa is alive and functioning as an indigenous culture.

So the root of the problem is Africa. Africa must take the middle course. At present, [Africa] tends toward Japan's way—to become Western (Western aim). This comes from the African's belief in the unquestioned superiority of the West and unquestioned uselessness of his own institutions. Both beliefs are completely *wrong*.

As Background suggests, [there are] other living cultures of great importance. I select Chinese as the most antithetical to Western and closest to African, but there are others—Hindu, Arabic, Iranic, Hebraic, Malayan—all of which at some time have touched the *African*.

But Africans must know about and appreciate the fact that even today the Western society has certainly conquered the world politically and economically. No argument. (See Toynbee: *A Study of History*.)

Publicity photograph, 1930s

With Peggy Ashcroft as
Desdemona in *Othello*, London,
1930

Consider the American Indian who has perished; Japan who after resisting has taken it all—and middle ground seems possible. China will probably take this middle ground—she will take creations of modern science but will carefully and cautiously adapt [them] to her own culture.

So borrowed from [the] West will be mainly applied science, with [the] culture and ideology-philosophy of [the] West rejected. It's my belief that even an ideology as strong and fanatical as communism may later disappear into the deeper roots of Chinese philosophy. I cannot see China Western or really accepting an ideology based upon Western metaphysics.

Superiority of Western culture is purely "technical"—Japan's rise in a few years demonstrates this completely. As I have indicated, in other phases of man's activities—in those deeper processes of man's psyche, those of feelings and intuition and will as opposed to those of the narrowly intellectual and knowledgeable, the other cultures of man's history (Grecian, Hindu, Syrian, Chinese) were and are much further developed. So [the] African must look [in] both directions, as his geographical position suggests. In his deeper processes he must look Eastward. For the technical and mechanical needs, to [the] West. Some adjustment must be made—some compromise. He cannot remain a museum piece as American Indian or Polynesian peoples; he must continue. Neither can he sell his *soul*. He can do it if he realizes there are many values elsewhere than in [the] West, and his own institutions are most valuable foundation of all....

...The fundamental need [is for] Africans to be proud of being black—and faith in his own institutions to lead him. Even the comparison with the Chinese serves only to give him courage to follow his own way. He can't be Chinese, Arabian, European or anything else. He must be African....

...Man's final destiny, when all technique is applied, is to live this inner existence—which is close enough to hidden mystery. Certainly it is the right path if the final mystery is to be solved. Scientific method, logical thought, rules of reason, science of words, and mathematical formulas have severe limitations and touch but one side of man's multifarious existence. The African, if he follows his destiny, will contribute much to that higher apprehension—for that has been his way for untold centuries.

...Surely in America and in the Western world, the Negro has become European thru force of circumstance; but then, speaking in a broad sense, he is a decadent cut off from his source. [For Westerners], nothing [is] more important than to explain that a Chinese immigrant is an *American*, and that therefore all *Chinese* should be European. No; Africa is there as China is there, and he [the Negro] has developed in his way just as distinctive a life and point of view—as Arabia is different; as ancient Egypt was different. To talk of making [an] African a European is to talk of making Asia European. Thus, the Negro question is confusing mainly because of the American Negro who has had center of stage. He is important only insofar as he represents an African heritage and gives and receives inspiration from that source.

Three ways exist for him [to be] *American*. Either in time to disappear into [the] great American mass (which [the] Negro prefers, frankly), which is [the] simple way—give up and disappear as [a] race altogether. Seems to me spineless and unthinkable. Remain [an] oppressed group, servile—also unthinkable. [Or] to become, as the Jew before him, a self-respecting, solid racial unit with its spiritual roots back in Africa whence he came. Not whining for this or that, but developing his powers to [the] point where there is no possible denial of equality. That can never be allowed by imitating a third-rate European culture....

Portrait of Paul Robeson as
Emperor Jones, by Edward
Steichen, 1933
(Courtesy of Joanna Steichen)

The following two excerpts, titled "Nationalism" and "Materialism," are from 1935 drafts written as rebuttals to arguments made by Norman Leys, an English physician and socialist scholar, in several discussions he had with Robeson on the relationship between African and Western cultures.

I am not a nationalist...I am more profoundly impressed by likenesses in cultural forms which seem to me to transcend the boundaries of nationality.

Whatever be the Social and Economic content of the culture—Archaic, Clan or Tribal organization; Feudalism, Capitalism, or Socialism—this cultural form seems to persist and to be of vital importance to the people concerned.

I realize that I am one of the very few who persists in suggesting that the African cultural form is in many respects similar to the old Archaic Chinese—before Confucius and Lao-tse. This form is the parent of the philosophies or systems of ethics of these two great sages; today it still reaches deep down into the Chinese soul and genius, as witness

With African students in London, 1936

the cultural basis of myth, clan cults, ritual, and ancestral beliefs. This comparison may seem much clearer if you will contrast this old Chinese form with an African form of a high level—namely, that of the Yoruba (Benin), Ashanti, Zulu, or Buganda.

Or, as a Chinese comparison, consider the tribal societies of South-Western China.

In the same way, I suggest that the form of many of the hitherto tribal societies of Northern, Central, and Southern Asia may be contrasted with the cultural form of many Bantu peoples.

So, I am in no way exclusively "nationalist" in pursuing my line of enquiry, and I am interested in the problems which confront the Chinese people, as well as in those which concern, for example, Abyssinia.

To me, the time seems long past when people can afford to think exclusively in terms of national units. The field of activity is far wider.

Just as it seems that the social and economic foundation must be broadened to transcend national boundaries if the world is to prosper, so there seems to be a possible synthesis of, and on the other hand constant interplay between, related cultural forms.

Africa's geographic location appears to have symbolic significance. She stands between East and West, and in the future must take from both. No matter what portion of the social and economic content of [the African's] future culture must come from the West and North, those facets which are specifically related to his cultural form (shaped in the distant past and still vigorous in spite of the impact of

With John Kenyatta on the set of *Sanders of the River*, 1934.

Still from the film *The Emperor Jones, 1933*

many foreign cultures and civilizations) will best be fed from the East, especially from the Central Asiatic Republics [of the Soviet Union] and China.

✴

The Materialism to which I refer in talking about Western Europe is this: The scale of values which places the acquisition of property above all else makes possession of material comforts an end in itself, and not a means to the development of the more intangible aspects of a culture. It creates a varied external life, but does little to cause the growth of a deep "inner life within the people of the society or culture."...If I use the words "spiritual" and "material," I do not mean to use the former in a religious, mystic sense. I refer to the contrast between the inner life of the artist (Bach, for example), and the external activity of the merchant who is concerned with selling his goods.

Western European man, in his striving for truth as the highest goal of man's activities, stumbled upon Western science. This science worked miracles, and, naturally, knowledge (and, through knowledge, power over the *external* world) became the most important and the most valuable good—the measure of all things.

In many cultures, however, with a different social structure and different values, the emphasis has been otherwise. According to a modern Chinese writer, Chinese philosophy has, from antiquity, sought an answer to the following question: "How can man become good?" The problem is not one of knowledge but of ethics—proceeding from the *will*, not the *intellect*, in the narrow sense of the old psychological divisions.

Because of the social structure of his society, the question above has also deeply occupied the African, as witness the extraordinary aptness of his proverbs [which are] intended to be morally persuasive, not intellectually knowledgeable. The African, in adapting himself to his environment, has also made great use of the third old division of the *Human Mind*, the *Emotions*— the domain of feeling. And what he has discovered may someday be of profound importance in the future Psychological and Sociological sciences.

...Great use of Emotional Forces and Processes seems also to have characterized the archaic culture of the Chinese—that period which antedates Confucius and Lao-tse. There is much to be learned from the experiences of these and other Eastern peoples which can be of inestimable value— especially in ethics, in Art, and in that aspect of pure science which depends upon the intuitive flash as a starting point or integrating point of departure.

As the culmination of his cultural studies, Robeson focused his attention on developing a cultural world view from the standpoint of the positive cultural development of the American Negro. The following excerpt is titled: "Must Be Proud of Being Negro" (1936)

I am a singer and an actor. I am primarily an *artist*. Had I been born in Africa, I would have belonged, I hope, to that family which sings and chants the glories and legends of the tribe. I might have been a priest. I would have liked, in my mature years, to have been a wise elder, for I worship wisdom and knowledge of the ways of men.

Naturally, I will touch upon economic and political problems, but for me these problems are part of a broader one without which no real problem of the black man can be solved—the belief of the black man, the African, in himself. And when I use the term African, I mean people of African descent the world over....For no person of African descent can escape the responsibility of Africa. The bond is one not only of race, but more important of culture—of attitudes to life, a way of living. In every black man flows the rhythm of Africa—it has taken different forms in America, in the Caribbean, in South America, but the base of all these expressions is Africa.

To me, that black man who claims to be essentially American, English, French, Spanish, is deluding himself. The very attempt to be a half-dozen nationalities at once proves the absurdity of the claim. Put us all together...and no one can tell whence the other comes. A chap one would swear was an African, comes from Jamaica. A chap one would wager comes from Chicago or Trinidad, comes from West Africa or East Africa, and so on.

Here, scattered over the world, are perhaps 75 million of African descent, able to give material and spiritual aid to their motherland, who spend their time disclaiming any relationship and trying to be this or that nationality—trying in the face of unchangeable bonds of color to override the disability and become white, Hindu, brown, yellow, anything but black. It's my humble opinion that we can get nowhere until we are proud of being black—and by the same token demand the respect of other people. For no one respects a man who does not respect himself.

...We can look to other cultures for aid,...[but we] must think for ourselves; [we] must find [an] African form.... In no part of [the] world will we ever be important as isolated individuals. [We] must represent a unity, a people, a culture, a form of our own. It's there—and strange to say we are being forced to keep it, as the Jews are theirs.... We'll have to, whether we like it or not.

...To the African who has not had contact in this part of the world, [it is our] duty to tell him: "America is not as pretty as it looks." Virtual slavery in the South—Negro's life of no value. The Scottsboro case is one of many to prove it.

The African will have to help *himself*. Neither Russia, Japan, England, France or any other nation will save the Black man. He will save himself. Since this is so—if we didn't have a common cultural tie, we'd have to create one. We are many different colors. [I] suppose we are as different culturally as the Hindu from the Chinese, or the American Indian from the Turk. But we have a common culture of real value, a simple culture but an integrated one quite to be distinguished from primitive civilization....

...Those of us who are friendly to Russia, as a country with no color prejudice and a country in which a Negro can live in terms of complete equality, see her future inextricably bound up with destiny of Asiatic mainland. I suggest that the African—and again I mean Africans the world over—study not only at the Sorbonne, Oxford, Cambridge, but also at the Universities of Peking, Wuhan, Shanghai, Moscow, Tokyo, Constantinople, Mexico City, Calcutta, Ceylon, Palestine, for our future is linked with that of the East. We must know them. The fight is for world *markets*. Those markets are in Asia and Africa.

We can be of no use as individuals here and there, whether as Nationalists, Socialists, Communists, Fascists—of one kind or another...

We must support Liberia and Haiti—two Negro Republics—and look to other spheres of freedom for the Black man. We must somehow find a united African people—perhaps not a national expression but a Federated expression —reflecting many sides but the sides of one basic black-African culture. I rest the bond more upon this cultural bond—this feeling, this spontaneity, this virile expression which marks the black man as African. I feel so happy to have found this culture.

I am interested in what happens in those parts of the world where there are not one or ten Negroes, but where there are millions.

What will happen to the vaunted freedom of London, Paris, Amsterdam, Brussels, if not one but 300,000 Negroes are admitted? What happens in England or France if 10,000,000 Negroes are present? What happens where these nations *do* rule millions of Negroes in the Congo and West Africa and South America?

Since in Russia the difference is class and not color, what happens if 100,000,000 Indians and American bourgeois Negroes and rich peasants of Africa go there. Naturally, they must suffer the fate of other non-proletarian classes. We face facts. Even from Russia's viewpoint, to convert 200,000,000 black people to Socialism by concentrating on individuals is hopeless. Russia is Socialist because they [Russians] took over a Tsarist state and made it what it is. Italy and Germany and Austria are Fascist because they took over a state, a nation, and as the government in power transformed the country to their ends.

So with American Negroes—[The Russians'] concern would be to make America Socialist. And a black Rich Peasant or Bourgeois is as much an enemy as a white one, and a white worker of the South is a friend as [much as] the Black middle class is an enemy. Millions of Negroes are middle class and rich peasants—or at least peasants with attachment to land as individual or clan property. So there is no place for any black man in any European country without some condition.

As obvious as these things are, interests of many kinds keep us blind. I was myself until about two years ago, when I began to study about Africa, meet Africans, and realize my position not only as that of an artist individual but as a black man of African heritage—one of millions of oppressed black people in different parts of the world.

And I began to think not white but black. And when I say black, I mean black....

"I Know a Lot About Fascism"

In the early years of the Cold War, the U. S. Government began a systematic and extensive campaign to identify, expose and silence Americans suspected of or known to have communist sympathies. Paul Robeson was one of the first to be subjected to this harassment. During 1950-1958, his passport was revoked and he was blacklisted in this country. This excerpt from his complete testimony under oath before the Joint Fact-Finding Committee on Un-American Activities in California on October 7, 1946 reveals his grace and dignity under pressure, as well as his sense of humor, even in difficult circumstances. The questioners were Senator Jack B. Tenney, chairman, and Richard E. Combs, committee counsel.

BY CHAIRMAN TENNEY:

Q: Will you state your full name, Mr. Robeson?
A: Paul Robeson.

Q: Where do you reside, Mr. Robeson?
A: I reside in Enfield, Connecticut.

Q: And your occupation?
A: I would say actor and singer, concert artist.

Q: Are you presently employed?
A: Certainly.

Q: All right, Mr. Combs. By the way, by whom are you employed, Mr. Robeson?
A: I am employed by the Metropolitan Music Bureau, which is a section of Columbia Concerts Bureau headed by Mr. Judson and Mr. Shang.

Q: I am sure we have all enjoyed your singing very much, Mr. Robeson.
A: Thank you.

BY MR. COMBS:

Q: Mr. Robeson, I understand you have to get to San Diego shortly after lunch?
A: Yes, I have to.

Q: For that reason we called you a little out of order at this time.
A: Well, thank you so much.

Q: The prime purpose, Mr. Robeson, in having you come before the committee is to ask you concerning the organization of certain groups that the committee has in the past been interested in, so that the examination will be pretty much limited to that—
A: Quite.

Q: So that you will know what our purpose is. By way of background, Mr. Robeson, you have been a concert singer and actor for a good many years, have you?
A: Since 1922 or 1923...

Q: Have you made several trips to the Soviet Union in connection with your profession?
A: I went to Europe the first time in 1922, to England, and I have been several times to the Soviet Union, both professionally and nonprofessionally.

Paul Robeson singing in the Hall of Columns, Moscow, USSR, June 1949

Q: When were you last there, Mr. Robeson?
A: I was last there about the end of 1937, the beginning of 1938.

Q: Are you familiar with a book written by Earl Browder who at that time was general secretary of the Communist Party of the United States, entitled *Communism in the United States*?
A: At what time was that, Mr. Combs?

Q: 1935.
A: No.

Q: It is nothing along a subversive line. It simply deals with one of your trips to the Soviet Union.
A: All right.

Q: The quote is... "Paul Robeson was greeted in Moscow as an honored guest of the Soviet Union. He sang in the biggest state theaters in Moscow and declared to the newspapers his great pleasure at the comradely reception accorded him in the Soviet Union, the like of which he had received nowhere else." Did you ever authorize Mr. Browder to make such a statement in his book?
A: No.

Q: You never heard of it before?
A: No.

Q: You don't know how it originated?
A: No.

Q: You are entirely unfamiliar with it?
A: That is right.

Q: Did you appear in the State Theater in Moscow in the early part of 1935 or the latter part of 1934?
A: I did, and in many theaters throughout the Soviet Union.

Q: So the information as to your being there is correct?
A: Of course.

Q: But the rest of the statement you know nothing about?
A: I know nothing about it. However, I did receive a fine reception.

Q: Yes.
A: As I have in many other countries of the world.

Q: I know you have. Mr. Robeson, of what does your family consist?
A: It consists of a wife, a son, brother and sister, and many cousins.

Q: Was your son educated in the Soviet Union?
A: He was in the Soviet Union from the time he was 8 until he was about 12.[1] And then as war began, as the rumors of war began in Europe in 1939—I was at that time living in London—he came back to London. And as he was in one of the Soviet schools, he was allowed by Mr. Maisky, at that time Soviet Ambassador in London, to attend a Soviet school in London. So he continued his Soviet education in London about another year and a half. So he has had what I would call a very basic Soviet education.

Q: Is he a citizen of the Soviet Union?
A: He is not. He was born in the United States.

Q: And he has retained his citizenship as you have?
A: That is right. He is now at Cornell [University] and in the American Army, as a matter of act.

Q: Mr. Robeson, are you acquainted with a man by the name of Festus

Coleman?

A: Festus Coleman. I visited him once in San Quentin I think.

Q: In San Quentin?
A: In San Quentin.

Q: In this state?
A: That is right. I was a member of a committee; at least the committee asked me to go out and see him. Evidently, looking at the photostats, it seemed there was a very grave miscarriage of California justice as far as I could see.

Q: He was convicted of an offense some years ago, was he not?
A: That is right; and, according to the committee, not proved at all.

Q: And your sole affiliation with that particular committee—I think it was the Free Festus Coleman Committee, wasn't it?
A: That is right.

Q: Your sole interest in affiliating with that committee was to see that the alleged miscarriage of justice was rectified, was it?
A: That is right.

Q: You had no personal acquaintance with Festus Coleman prior to that time?
A: None whatsoever.

Q: Is he still in San Quentin, do you know?
A: I think so, as far as I know. I don't know.

Q: Does the Committee to Free Festus Coleman still exist? Is it active?
A: I don't know. I trust so. I trust so.

Q: Are you still affiliated with it?
A: I wasn't affiliated with it, but if they ask me to speak for it again, I will certainly do so, because I believed at the time and still believe there was a miscarriage of justice.

Q: But you never actually affiliated with the committee?
A: No. I was just asked to speak.

Q: Are you acquainted with Charlotta Bass?
A: Oh, surely, yes.

Q: You have known her for a number of years?
A: Yes.
Q: She was active through the columns of her paper, *The California Eagle*, in Mr. Coleman's behalf?
A: I am sure she was. I consider her one of the outstanding journalists of our people.

Q: Do you know Revels Cayton?
A: He is currently—we are working together in the National Negro Congress.

Q: Now, there are two organizations, comparable organizations, are there not, for the benefit of the colored peo-

With son Paul, Jr. at home in Enfield, CT, 1941 (photograph by Frank Bauman)

Robeson singing at San Quentin Prison, 1941

ple: the National Negro Congress, to which you referred; and isn't there also an organization known as the National Association for the Advancement of Colored People, too?

A: It isn't current. It has been long established, and it has done great service.

Q: Is it still in existence?

A: Oh, I should say so.

Q: Are you affiliated with both of them?

A: Yes, I work for them.

Q: Are you a member of the Independent Citizens' Committee of the Arts, Sciences and Professions?

A: I am, of the executive committee.

Q: Locally?

A: No; that is, from New York.

Q: You know of an organization called the Joint Anti-Nazi Refugee Committee?

A: Yes.

Q: Just what is that? Will you tell us briefly what the organization is and its purpose?

A: As far as I know, it was a committee formed like other relief organizations. We had the Russian Relief. You had relief for many countries. This was a relief organization for the Republican Spaniards, the people who fought against Franco. I might also add that from England in 1937 and 1938 I went to Republican Spain to sing for the Spanish Republicans in what I would call the first onslaught of fascism by Franco. It has been documented. President Roosevelt was very clear about that. The democracies made a very horrible mistake in not supporting Democratic Spain, and for that matter I think they are making a terrible mistake in supporting Franco. At the time of my visit—

Q: When was that?

A: The end of 1937—Mr. Clement Attlee,[2] head of the British Government, went with me. At that time he understood (*laughter*).

Q: The committee is drawing no implication that there was anything wrong in your going there.

A: I understand.

Q: There seems to be some feeling there.

A: I understand.

Q: Are you an officer or were you ever an officer in that committee?

A: No. My general work has been of a kind just recently—I felt many, many years ago—I was in London in 1933 at the beginning of the Hitler regime in Germany, and my first concerts were to aid Jewish refugees who came from Germany to London, and I played in the theaters for them. At that time artists felt they were a little apart from the struggle. I myself have never been, because at Rutgers when I played on the football field I felt I was struggling for the Negro people, my people, and I was conscious of the struggle.

I began to sing. I was just an artist coming and giving my services. That was more or less the general pattern, that I go and sing and act and raise funds to help people and organizations and causes that I think are worthwhile. Only recently have I come on the board of directors and have been sort of chairman of some committees; because, after all, in the struggle that I think still goes on—I hate to say this— I think this is one of the evidences of the struggle that still goes on, because I have watched the work of the committee from afar,[3] and I believe that sometimes it may be on the wrong track. But as a part of that struggle I have had to take further part, and I will continue to, I feel, until fascism is completely destroyed.

Singing to Republican troops outside Madrid, Spain during the Spanish Civil War, 1938 (photograph by Eslanda Robeson)

And whatever—I heard some of the remarks this morning—our hopes for American democracy and democracies in other parts of the world, as a Negro in America who is also heading a crusade against lynching, where one-tenth of the citizens are being shut out without redress or even a formal statement from the President of our United States; I know a lot about fascism, and I know what it means because I have seen it, I have helped fight it. I helped the Norwegians and many other people, the Danes and Frenchmen and Spaniards to fight against fascism. I know what it is. So I might have to participate a great deal more.

Q: You have been active against it for many years?
A: That is right.

CHAIRMAN TENNEY:
May I interrupt? We heard that lynching and things that were mentioned, that this committee deplores and condemns. . .
A: Yes.

Q: . . .long before we had the term fascism.
A: That is right.

Q: The term has been so loosely used because of the recent rise of Hitler that it has almost become synonymous with certain groups as meaning anti-Communist. You don't use it in that sense?
A: Oh, no.

Q: We recognize those abuses.
A: That is certainly one of its elements, that it would be.

Q: We recognized those things in the South before the rise of Mussolini or Hitler.
A: Quite true. I was trying to explain to the President the other day, and suggested maybe Nuremberg [trials of Nazi war criminals] was responsible for the South, but [he] thought not.[4] I am glad you agree with me.

Q: I didn't get that connection myself.
A: No.

Q: You are pointing out abuses?
A: That is right. It doesn't matter what name they are called. I agree we should not use names because to me—fascism—one of the things we don't want is the superiority of one group over another and their right to kill another group or wipe them out like they did in Germany. Call it what you will. We happen to call fascism what the German people did to the Jewish people. I don't like to use names myself.
Q: It is the beast or something that arises in certain types of people?

A: No. I say it is the kind—I would put it this way: It is the necessity of action of a certain kind of minority when their interests are threatened, as they were in Franco Spain; the big landowners, for example; the big businessmen in France—the 400 families who handed the French people over to Hitler and Fascism. And so, for example, in the State of California, there are big interests, big powerful interests—oil and fruit interests who are mobilizing...their forces to do exactly what happened in the South, or what happened in Germany, if they were challenged by people who wanted a decent wage—as I see on the streets over here.

Q: It wouldn't be your contention, Mr. Robeson, merely because a man had a financial interest, being in the category of being a capitalist, that he would necessarily condone the things we are talking about?
A: He wouldn't condone them, but he might have to do them if his interests are threatened. For example, in France I met nice Frenchmen. I have friends among them. I have friends I played football with who are big bankers in America today. They hated Roosevelt. They hate labor. They would have 20,000,000 unemployed. They are nice guys. We grew up together, but today they feel they would have to bear down on labor as firmly as they did in certain parts of Fascist Europe. And I feel what is going on right here in Los Angeles is the same thing.

Q: You had that same misunderstanding from . . . in the middle of 1941.
A: Yes.

Q: In which, for instance, the Communist Party picketed the White House and called Roosevelt a warmonger. We have the statements of a certain Writers Congress held in New York in which they likened Roosevelt to Hitler and Mussolini.

A: Well, no.

Q: You don't mean to tell the committee, I am sure...
A: No...

Q:...that merely because a man is a capitalist and has some money...
A: No...

Q: ...that he becomes a lyncher or would condone those things?
A: No. I was giving a definition of fascism; that it is not necessarily the beast in man; it is the necessity of certain groups to protect their interests, like a former witness said, against social change, that is all. They want the status quo or even much less than that. That was the essence of fascism. When people in Europe were pressing forward to social change, the Fascists said No and beat them back. I feel that is a part of what is going on maybe in our country today; the fight against Roosevelt was a fight against social change within our system.

Q: I may be going far afield here. . .but, are you a member of the Communist Party? (*Laughter.*) I ask it of everybody, so don't feel embarrassed.
A: No. I am not embarrassed. I have heard it so much. Every reporter has asked me that. I will certainly answer it, Mr. Tenney. Only you might ask me if I am a member of the Republican or Democratic Party. As far as I know, the Communist Party is a very legal one in the United States. I sort of characterize myself as an anti-fascist and independent. If I wanted to join any party, I could just as conceivably join the Communist Party, more so today than I could join the Republican or Democratic Party. But I am not a Communist.

Q: You are not? I suppose from your statement, would I be proper and correct in concluding that you would be more sympathetic with the Communist Party than with the Republican or Democratic Party?

A: I would put it this way: I said I could join either one of them just as well. In order to clear this up, my association with the Communists throughout the world and in America and working with citizen groups—take France, where it is documented, in Czechoslovakia where I visited as a singer, or in Norway—I found that among people over there fighting against Hitler, that the first people to die, the first people to sacrifice, and the first people who understood the struggle [against fascism] were Communists. So they were elected to great power in France. I was in Czechoslovakia singing for American troops. The Czech people are a very democratic people, even in the words of Mr. Churchill. I saw they elected the Communists to power. So I have no reason to be inferring communism is evil or that someone should run around the corner when they hear it, as I heard here this morning, because today Communists are in control or elected by people because of their sacrifice in much of the world. I feel that Americans have got to understand it unless they want to drop off of the planet. They have got to get along with a lot of Communists...

...We have the American way of life, and they have a dictatorship; and the best way, as I said before, is to oppose it with our democracy. We can oppose this by giving freedom to the people who don't have it in our country. We don't need to go to war to decide which way of life is to be chosen. I believe the Soviet Union wants to build their life within one-sixth of the world's surface where they are.

Q: You mean we should lead by example?

A: That is right. And whatever happens, whatever our different ways of life, we can solve them within the framework of peace. I think this is guaranteed...

... As a Negro I sit here today, but I can go down in Georgia and be dead tomorrow. I am only saying there may be different ways of life in the world. Marxism was not created in Russia. It began perhaps as a scientific thing, began with the Chartists in the English industrial revolution. This was an English idea, and Marx took it over. Like we went from Fourierism to our own way of life, Marx examined society. He did not make it up. We did not

Snapshot, late 1940s

make up the clash between the poor people in Spain and Franco.

BY CHAIRMAN TENNEY:

Q: But Mr. Robeson, he took his philosophy from Hegel, trying to prove the superiority of Prussian culture. They both wanted to prove certain things and went all the way back to Greece to prove it.
A: You are going into a philosophical discussion. That is sort of a philosophy if you will. Hegel believed in the idea, and the material thing; that is something else. But the structure of Marxism which we are concerned with and struggles of the peoples to take power, like in Russia, came from Marx's examination of the material structure of society.

Q: Speaking of California...

MR. COMBS:
May I finish my line of questioning?

CHAIRMAN TENNEY:
This fits right in.

MR. COMBS: All right.

CHAIRMAN TENNEY: One question and I will finish, briefly. In answer to these matters, you refer to Georgia and the South.
A: Yes.

Q: Compared to California, you don't find that sort of thing, or do you, in California?
A: You see, again, one of the essences of fascism—to come back again to the word, and we shouldn't call them words—one of the things most important in my struggle, and one of the things I have had to work out with the Negro people: you had these insults and the things that happened to the Negro. So I grew up and had these insults, and things happened to me as a Negro, and I grew tense about them. But then when I got to London I found that they were driving the Jewish people all over the world, and I found, strange to say, the Welsh miner was just as bad off as the Negro down in Georgia, and the same things were happening to him. So the thing I have been impressed with was this: I saw there is one struggle.

Yes, in California; let me tell you what happened to me in California.

BY MR. COMBS: At Vanessi's? [a restaurant.]

A: Don't go into that. Just last year, for example—that is all right—I am up in Fresno and I was amazed. It isn't just Negroes. This was really extraordinary to see people like Armenians—to be an Armenian, it is almost as bad as being a Negro. This is really fantastic. We went into a restaurant near there with a relative of William Saroyan. They said: "We are not serving people." People sitting around. I said: "But you are serving. It is four o'clock in the afternoon."

He said: "What do you mean coming in here with your hat on with white folks?" Like I say, my boy would have examined the incident and smiled, but I started for the guy and he started to reach [for a gun]. And they said no, and somebody said for me to be careful; so I said O.K. But in Fresno, California, I could have been dead exactly like I would have been dead in Georgia. I am not saying the state of California wouldn't have done more about it, but I would have been good and dead. (*Laughter.*)

I walked out again in the fruit fields, and I saw Mexicans, you see, Mexican workers. Now I say to my mind—you have been through this before with groups (*laughter*)—I saw great inequalities in the State of California, tremendous inequalities. And I still see the struggle that went on in the time of Roosevelt; not so sharp, but the same struggles I see abroad. I still see in the state of California the fight of tremendously powerful interests against a guy getting a decent wage— the kind of war we fight to see that he gets it. The way not to worry about all of these changes being too fast…is really to give this guy a chance. Roosevelt did that.

I think American big businessmen feel that they are going to crack down all over the country and go back to the same old-fashioned idea of imperialism, making this an American century and going back to Mexico if necessary and taking the oil. To my way of feeling, you can't keep people starving and one-third of the people underprivileged. That is the way I see the Negro struggle in the South. The white worker is just as bad off. We know what went on in the South after the Civil War. I see the struggle as the unified struggle of the Negro and white workers, divided because the fellows at the top keep them divided; but their essential interests are the same.

There is no solution to the Negro problem except by working it out together, and the Negro people must look to the people who are in that position; that affects me. Although I have been personally successful, I have poor sharecroppers down the list [i.e., relatives], and I could be poor overnight and have to go back to [ordinary] work. I worked very hard as a child. My father was a slave. So all my life's interest has been with people who have been suppressed, and I know the Negro struggle intimately.

I feel the guy down low, whether he knows it or not, has got to be on my side…. So I will fight with the CIO[5] and help white workers or white liberals…There are just a few guys—they maybe good fellows, as I say, but their interests demand that they press things down. And this has led me to doing

the kind of things I do, and I do them at great sacrifice. Mr. Behymer[6] can be so upset by this [testimony] that he may cancel my appearance. Well, let him. I face these things, and I am willing to do it.

Q: You testified a moment ago about a comparison of the Soviet Union and other countries.
A: Yes.

Q: Is it your opinion that in October, 1917, when the [Bolshevik] revolution had its inception, that it would have been impossible to find a better country to test the principles of Marxism than Russia as it existed under the Czars?
A: No. I would say the best country in the world to test the principles of Marxism might be the America of today, with the wealth and so forth.

Q: Yes, but I am speaking of 1917.
A: I would say it was not a good test because Russia was too poor.…

———————

1. Actually, Paul Robeson, Jr. was there for about a year and a half, from age 9 until age 10 and a half.

2. Labor Prime Minister of England in 1947 and a leading supporter of the Cold War, who had been a prominent left-winger in 1937.

3. He means the committee before which he is testifying.

4. Two weeks earlier, Robeson had suggested to President Truman that Southern lynchers should be treated like the Nazi war criminals.

5. Congress of Industrial Organizations

6. The producer of Robeson's scheduled appearance in San Diego.

Speaking at a civil rights meeting, Madison Square Garden, 1949.

Trouble in Peekskill

On August 27, 1949, rioters blocked a concert Paul Robeson had scheduled in Peekskill, New York. Concert goers were attacked— Paul Robeson and Larry Brown escaped the mob when their driver saw what was happening and sped away. Three days later, Robeson responded to the riot in a speech he gave at Harlem's Golden Gate Ballroom. He was introduced by Benjamin J. Davis, Jr., Negro city councilman from Harlem, who was also a leader of the U.S. Communist Party. His remarks were frequently interrupted by wild applause, cheers and shouts.

Well, as Ben said, they've got their answer here tonight. I don't notice any [American] Legion around here. But I know, as you know, that this is a very historic moment in American life. I'm going to say a few words later. But to me it means a real turn in the anti-Fascist struggle in America. There is no citizen of our land of any kind who doesn't realize what that meant in Peekskill the other night. I've met them all over the streets, up and down-town, people of all walks of life. They understand that when that can happen in Peckskill, it can happen to any other American.

We are part of a very historic departure. This means that from now on we take the offensive. *WE* take it! We'll have our meetings and our concerts all over these United States. (*Applause, shouts.*) That's right. And we'll see that our women and our children are not harmed again! We will understand that, like here tonight, the surest way to get that police protection is to have it very clear that we'll protect ourselves, and good!

I want you to know that I've been up and down this America before. I've been to Memphis, Tennessee; to Florida; to Georgia; all over these United States. And I'll be back in Peekskill—all over these United States. And I'll be there—to sing for audiences wherever I can find them. That's right.

But I want to thank you for this assemblage tonight—for what it means up and down the streets of Harlem. As I say, there are a few things I wanted to say. I've written out a few pages. Before I go any further, I have my old stalwart friend here—we grew up here together, from different parts of America. And you know, we artists—we've traveled all over the world. Brownie [Lawrence Brown] is a pianist of the greatest distinction, one of the finest artists not only in the United States but in the world. (*Applause*)

And where was he the other night? Well, we were sitting in the same car right in front of that gateway. And he's here tonight, and he's with me all the time. And I can't ever tell him—I try to tell him once in a while, never sort of face to face, but to audiences like you, who love him, that I know our lives have been close. He knows how I feel—that as long as I can sing a note, as long as we're going along, we're going to be there together. And that he, coming from Florida, suffering deeply in his youth, is proud of an audience like this and knows that for him—and he's helping you all the time—that you're going to make an America and a Florida where he can go back one day and be proud of being an American in the greatest and finest traditions of our land. (*Applause*)

Eugene Bullard, the only black World War I fighter pilot, being beaten by police as he tries to enter the second Robeson Peekskill concert, September 4, 1949 (Courtesy of *People's Weekly World*)

[Paul then sings "Go Down Moses"; enthusiastic applause]

The next is one that comes from the aftermath of slavery, and it leads me close to my own history and to my own father. The other day, the head of the Veterans of Foreign Wars, a Mr. Lewis, suggested that he would buy me a one-way ticket to the Soviet Union. As nice as that would be *(laughter, applause)*, there's another job to do. I have one ancestor who was a slave and freed himself—became a Quaker in Southern New Jersey near Pennsylvania, and as a baker baked a lot of the bread that the troops of George Washington ate when they crossed the Delaware.

But my father was a slave; and his father was a slave, just as were millions of the Negro people brought to this land, and to the West Indies, and to Latin America. As I have said many times, on their backs and by their blood was created much of the early wealth of this land, that made this a great America. And by their blood I'll stay here, and I'll fight for my freedom and the freedom of my people.

Back in those terrible times—just on the edge, when they saw freedom around the corner, still in slavery; when they said: "No more pcck of corn for me—no, you won't sell me for that any more; no more pint of salt for me; no more driver's lash for me." And that's all I'm saying—to the Klan, to the

Paul Robeson with Howard Fast, writer, and William Patterson, head of the Civil Rights Congress, at press conference following the September 4, 1949 Robeson concert at Peekskill, NY (*Courtesy of People's Weekly World*)

Legionnaires, to big business, even to the chief executive of these United States! The Negro people say, "No more driver's lash for me! Give us some freedom! Give us some democracy! That's all!"

[*Paul sings "No More Auction Block For Me"; thunderous applause*]

It's awful hot and everything, but when I'm with my own folks like this, it feels good; so I'm alright. (*Warm applause, shouts*)

This is one that I'm dedicating—"Scandalize My Name," you've heard me sing it—to this wonderful "Free Press" that runs up and down this land. You know what I mean. (*Laughter*) And they overdo it a little every once in a while. I was on the avenue the other day. You know, we read these newspapers and always think they tell the truth. So I saw an old friend of mine from way back. He started to look at me, and he said: "Paul, you know that damn *News* ain't tellin' the truth!" (*Laughter*) "Well," I said, "How did you find that out?" He said: "Trying to take a picture and pervert the truth; they ain't kiddin' nobody!" So they'll have to watch it—watch out for those pictures there, fellas!" (*Laughter, applause.*)

[*Paul sings "Scandalize My Name." Audience sings last verse with him; joyful applause, shouts*]

This is Bishop Lawson; I was down at his church the other day, and he asked me—(*applause, cheers*). He's a minister who asks for nothin', because he's a little too radical for these boys. (*Applause; requests for songs are shouted from audience*)

[*Paul then sings "Ol' Man River"; rising swell of sustained applause; shouts; ovation*]

It won't be a long while; just a few more—I just want to ask that we go

Buses and cars returning to New York City from the September 4, 1949 Robeson concert at Peekskill were stoned mercilessly by mobs while the police stood by (*Courtesy of People's Weekly World*)

home tonight and tell our neighbors. And I'm sure that the people of America will know about us tonight. That this has been shaped here and must continue. A united front, as I say, in the struggle for freedom in America. The working class, people of all groups—the Negro people, the Jewish people, the foreign born; the intellectuals—those who are among the great writers of our nation.

What a magnificent thing! How deeply I feel about Howard Fast! Knowing that he stood there, giving blow for blow, protecting the women and the children and protecting our freedom. (*Applause*) That's the kind of writer the working class is proud to hail! And I give my thanks to those brave 42 fellows who stood there arm-in-arm, holding off 500 to 1,000 Legionnaires. That's a measure of the cowardice of Fascism! That's the reason it has been beaten down wherever people have had the courage to mobilize…

…The other night they said this was Red. That the cross burned because of one person, because of Reds. It burned because they are afraid of the Negro people today. They can't answer for us in this so-called American democracy. They're afraid of the Jewish people—a people who suffered and died in the struggle against Fascism, and 600,000 strong created a new state against British and American imperialism; and they must join us in our struggle!

They are afraid of the working class of this nation. For when it comes to understanding what has happened—and this has helped them to understand—this was also aimed against the workers of America. They want cheap labor…. It's very simple. It has to do with tobacco and copper; yes, and oil and rubber. And we must get these markets to see that we are a wealthy nation. I say the President is quite right—I know these tobacco workers and those cotton workers just can't wait for those investments so they can get all that gravy. Yeah!

And he's talking about "We must develop the underdeveloped nations of the world. We must give them some equipment." That's right, Mr. President, the same kind of equipment you've been giving us for 300 years down there in the South. We've got a lot of equipment, a lot of those mines, plantations; so you go to Africa and help them develop, that's right. But they're catching on, just like the Chinese, you know. They're not having much of it.

…I want to say to my people not only in Harlem but all over the United States, it's been a long struggle that I've waged, sometimes not very well understood. But ever since I was a child, I've been conscious of my responsibility to the Negro people.

And I stand here tonight, I assure you, bringing you strength, the Negro people of this land, from millions of people all over the world. When I have fought for the British worker, it's because I've been trying to make him understand that he must fight for the African worker and for the West Indian worker—that the same people who beat him down beat down my folks in the West Indies and Africa. And this time when I was in England I had the pleasure of seeing Scotch miners stand at their pits and throw in two thousand dollars for black workers in Africa and the West Indies. And the Electrical-Trades Union just telegraphed me the other day that another thousand had gone in. And other thousands are going to go, because they understand, at last, that this unity of the white workers in Britain is one with the black workers all over the colonial world. And that's what these guys don't like.

And I was down in Jamaica and Trinidad.... I was down in the West Indies. I was talking to a man from the Negro press. They've got a Judd Bill. They don't want West Indians to come into America anymore. That's right. Because down there I found, in Jamaica, it's a little different, you see. We're sort of cooped in down South, though we've got a pretty good force there in the cotton belt, you know. Quite a few million there, and all together. Quite a few million—much more than that 600,000 in Israel. Quite a few million. And if they got a little rough one afternoon and got tired of being lynched, it wouldn't be so funny...

So we look for our allies—the working class—to see that we get some kind of rights. That's right, we'll fight for them constitutionally; fight for them absolutely parliamentarily. Just don't lynch us—you know what I mean! Just don't lynch us! We'll be very parliamentary about it.

Well now, down in Jamaica they tell me they don't know nothin' about that at all. And those white boys—sailors—came in. And I've met some nice sailors, you know. American boys, white fellows—from the South as a matter of fact. They must have been part of the progressive struggle. There's one thing you must remember: this is a common struggle, and we have allies among the white working class. I was in the South, and they stood side-by-side with Larkin Marshall and with Henry Wallace. And many a white Southerner came up to shake my hand and say: "Paul, we're gonna stand by your side, whatever happens. We're gonna fight it out together."

So this was the time that some of the Legionnaires I met the other night, I guess, were down in Jamaica. And they tell me they were a little rough in the early stages. They thought they were somewhere in some southern states—Mississippi, or Arkansas, or somewhere. Somewhere the Klan had been used to riding.

And they got a little rough. And those Jamaican boys tried to tell 'em: "Now, you better stay on that boat, you know...And they tell me that a couple of days later—they just wouldn't learn—man, the Atlantic Ocean was so full of things!

Paul Robeson in Stalingrad, USSR, June 1949

That's one thing that makes it a little hard for the West Indian people to understand us sometimes. You've got to understand that, you know. They're used to being kicked around, and they talk about it. So they want to come in here; they want to talk it up louder, see? But I thanked these people and my brothers and sisters who have come here to teach me to speak out for my freedom. And I'm with them, I'm telling you!

You must understand that in Nigeria, for example, there are thirty million Negroes today who may get their independence first. They will certainly get their independence very soon in the West Indies. We must fight for their liberation, because they're going to help to liberate us, I'm telling you.

...So that's the reason that I say—and I say it again: we must fight for peace; we must have nothing to do with a war in the interests of a few greedy profit-makers! And they can call me down to Washington tomorrow if they want to.

I will be loyal to the America of the true traditions; to the America of the Abolition, of Harriet Tubman, of Thaddeus Stevens, of those who fought for

Paul Robeson with friends in Stalingrad, USSR, June 1949

my people's freedom, not of those who tried to enslave them. I will have no loyalty to the Forrestals, to the Harrimans, to the Wall-Streeters, whom many a time on a football field I have beaten [*thumps lectern*], stepped on [*thumps lectern*], as if they were just any crackers [i.e., *southern racists*].

I want to thank you, as I say, in this Harlem and in America. I know it's been hard to understand. But it's a wonderful thing to walk on the avenue and have everybody say: "Hello Paul. Most of the time I'm with you. We can't quite speak out like you do, but we know what you're doin'." And maybe a couple of years ago he'd have said: "There goes Mr. Robeson. He's a nice singer. And he's fighting for us." But he wouldn't know anything about me.

Today he disagrees, so he says: "Paul, come in here. Let me get your side here; what're you talking about? What did Soviet Russia ever do for me?" I said: "Just wait a minute now. One thing they did for you—in destroying Fascism; you remember, you better remember this Hitler again. He destroyed six million Jewish people—burned six million Jewish people up. He was just hoping to get hold of ten or fifteen million Negroes to burn up. Well, the reason he couldn't get hold of them happened to be because ten to twenty million Russians took him. They took him."

And I was in Stalingrad, and I saw a letter in the museum from President Roosevelt saying to these Russian people in Stalingrad: "That's where civilization was saved."

...And the Russians happen to be the greatest force against those Rankins and plantation owners in Mississippi who would enslave our people. They can't be such a bad people—must be pretty smart, too. That in thirty years, since 1917, Russia has now come to be the nation of the world challenging the United States—*challenging the United States....*So somewhere let us understand all these things tonight: No Red-baiting. Unity in order to attain freedom. And, as I said, one has to grow; one has to learn every day. And what I've learned, I've brought all these allies, I feel, to the Negro people from all over the world. . . Evidently, I've got to get close to home. I've got to get close to the struggle. And there's nothing that could have drawn me closer to the Negro people again than trying to take me away from them, trying to destroy a whole lifetime of service to my people.

At reception during visit to Moscow, USSR, 1949

I want to thank you, and I want all my friends from years back to know—they're going to see plenty of me from now on. I'm here, and this is the base in the struggle for the freedom of my people in my time, not some hundreds of years hence. Any, any time, that you want to call on me, I'm in there fighting for my people. And I'll be there tonight, tomorrow night, and the day after tomorrow, and right on. Because you're with me; because we're all fighting together for the freedom, not only of the Negro people, but of an America which, years hence, our children can be proud of. We'll be proud we helped create an America where they could walk this earth with their shoulders back, full of the dignity of humankind.

[Then Paul went outside to speak briefly to the huge crowd assembled on the sidewalks and in the street]

Paul Robeson speaking at Paris Peace Conference, April 1949. There he made the highly controversial statement that it was unthinkable that American Negroes could go to war against the Soviet Union

Here I Stand

In 1958, a U.S. Supreme Court decision denied the State Department the right to revoke a citizen's passport on the basis of his political beliefs. Robeson resumed traveling internationally, both to perform and to participate in worthy social and political causes around the world. This excerpt from Chapter Five of his autobiography, published in 1958, is an eloquent argument not only for the civil and political rights of African-Americans, but also for the power of all people everywhere, united in a common and just cause.

THE POWER OF NEGRO ACTION

"How Long, O Lord, How Long?"—that ancient cry of the oppressed is often voiced these days in editorials in the Negro newspapers whose pages are filled with word-and-picture reports of outrages against our people. A photograph of a Negro being kicked by a white mobster brings the vicious blow crashing against the breast of the reader, and there are all the other horrible pictures—burning cross, beaten minister, bombed school, threatened children, mutilated man, imprisoned mother, barricaded family—which show what is going on.

How long? The answer is: *As long as we permit it.* I say that Negro action can be decisive. I say that we ourselves have the power to end the terror and to win for ourselves peace and security throughout the land. The recognition of this fact will bring new vigor, boldness and determination in planning our program of action and new militancy in winning its goals.

…The die-hard racists who shout "Never!" to equal rights, and the gradualists who mumble "Not now," are quite convinced that the Negro is powerless to bring about a different decision. Unfortunately, it is also true that to a large extent the Negro people do not know their own strength and do not see how they can achieve the goals they so urgently desire. The basis for this widespread view is obvious. We are a minority, a tenth of the population of our country. In all the terms in which power is reckoned in America—economic wealth, political office, social privilege—we are in a weak position; and from this the conclusion is drawn that the Negro can do little or nothing to compel a change.

It must be seen, however, that this is not a case of a minority pitting itself against a majority. If it were, if we wanted to gain something for ourselves by taking it away from the more powerful majority, the effort would plainly be hopeless. But that is not the case with our demand. Affirming that we are indeed created equal, we seek the equal rights to which we are entitled under the law. The granting of our demand would not lessen the democratic rights of the white people: on the contrary, it would enormously strengthen the base of democracy for all Americans. We ask for nothing that is not ours by right, and herein lies the great moral power of our demand. It is the admitted rightness of our claim which has earned for us the moral support of the majority of white Americans.

The granting of our demand for first-class citizenship, on a par with all others, would not in itself put us in a position of equality. Oppression has kept us on the bottom rungs of the ladder, and even with the removal of all barriers we will still have a long way to climb in order to catch up with the general standard of living. But the equal place to which we aspire cannot be reached without the equal rights we demand, and so the winning of those rights is not a maximum fulfillment but a minimum necessity, and we cannot settle for less. Our viewpoint on this matter is not a minority opinion in our country. Though the most rabid champions of "white superiority" are unwilling to test their belief by giving the Negro an equal opportunity, I believe that most white Americans are fair-minded enough to concede that we should be given that chance.

The moral support of the American majority is largely passive today, but what must be recognized—and here we see the decisive power of Negro action —is this: *Wherever and whenever we, the Negro people, claim our lawful rights with all of the earnestness, dignity and determination that we can demonstrate, the moral support of the American people will become an active force on our side.*

The most important part of the Little Rock story was not what Governor Faubus and the local mobs did, nor was it what President Eisenhower was

Paul Robeson with friends in Harlem, 1955
(*Courtesy of People's Weekly World*)

Paul Robeson on stage at his 1952 Peace Arch Park concert. The U.S. Immigration Service had previously prevented him from crossing the Canadian border to sing to the Canadian Union of Mine, Mill and Smelter Workers. He returned later that year to sing from U.S. soil to thousands of Canadians gathered just across the border

moved to do: the important thing was that nine Negro youngsters, backed by their parents, the Negro community and its leadership, resolved to claim their right to attend Central High School. The magnificent courage and dignity these young people displayed in making that claim won the admiration of the American public. Their action did more to win the sympathy and support of democratic-minded white people than all the speeches about "tolerance" that have ever been made.

Little Rock was but one of the first skirmishes in the battle to end Jim Crow schools; much greater tests of our determination will soon be at hand. The desegregation of public education is as yet only in the first stages, and the hard core of resistance has not been met. But there is no turning back, and the necessity to prepare ourselves for the struggles that lie ahead is urgent.

I have pointed to the sources of strength that exist at home and abroad. What power do we ourselves have?

We have the power of numbers, the power of organization, and the power of spirit. Let me explain what I mean.

Sixteen million people are a force to be reckoned with, and indeed there are many nations in the U.N. whose numbers are less. No longer can it be said that the Negro question is a sectional matter: the continuing exodus from the South has spread the Negro community to all parts of the land and has concentrated large numbers in places which are economically and politically the most important in the nation. In recent years much has been written about the strategic position of Negro voters in such pivotal states as New York, Ohio, Pennsylvania, Michigan, Illinois and California, but generally it can be said that the power of our numbers is not seen or acted upon. Let us consider this concept in connection with something that is apparent to all.

Very often these days we see photographs in the newspapers and magazines of a Negro family—the husband, wife, their children—huddled together in their newly purchased or rented home, while outside hundreds of Negro-haters have gathered to throw stones, to howl filthy abuse, to threaten murder and arson; and there may or may not be some policemen at the scene. But something is missing from this picture that ought to be there, and its absence gives rise to a nagging question that cannot be stilled: *Where are the other Negroes?* Where are the hundreds and thousands of other Negroes in that town who ought to be there protecting their own? *The power of numbers* that is missing from the scene would change the whole picture as nothing else could. It is one thing to terrorize a helpless few, but the forces of race hate that brazenly whoop and holler when the odds are a thousand to one are infinitely less bold when the odds are otherwise.

I am not suggesting, of course, that the Negro people should take law enforcement into their own hands. But we have the right and, above all, we have the duty, to bring the strength and support of our entire community to defend the lives and property of each individual family. Indeed, the law itself will move a hundred times quicker whenever it is apparent that the power of our numbers has been called forth. The time has come for the great Negro communities throughout the land—Chicago, Detroit, New York, Birmingham and all the rest—to demonstrate that they will no longer tolerate mob violence against one of their own. In listing the inalienable rights of man, Thomas Jefferson put *life* before *liberty, and the pursuit of happiness*; and it must be clear that for Negro Americans today the issue of *personal security* must be put first, and resolved first, before all other matters are attended to. When the Negro is told that he must "stay in his place," there is always the implicit threat that unless he does so, mob violence will be used against him. Hence, as I see it, nothing is more important than to establish the fact that we will no longer suffer the use of mobs against us. Let the Negro people of but a single city respond in an all-out manner at the first sign of a mob in mass demonstrations, by going on strike, by organizing boycotts, and the lesson will be taught in one bold stroke to people everywhere.

It was an excellent idea to call for a Prayer Pilgrimage for Freedom to assemble in Washington on May 17, 1957, the third anniversary of the Supreme Court decision, and the thousands who gathered there were inspired with a sense of solidarity and were deeply stirred by the speeches that were made. In terms of dignity and discipline the gathering was a matter for great pride. But there was at the same time a sense of disappointment at the size of the rally which did not, as a national mobilization, truly reflect the power of our numbers. Various charges were later made in the press, and heatedly denied, that important elements of leadership had "dragged their feet" in the preparations, but no constructive purpose would be served by going into those arguments here. The point I wish to make is this: When we call for such a mobilization again (and it ought to be done before another three years passes), we must go all-out to rally not tens of thousands but hundreds of thousands in a demonstration that will show we really mean business. And we should do more than listen to speeches and then go quietly home. Our spokesmen should go to the White House and to Congress and, backed by the massed power of our people, present our demands for action. Then they should come back to the assembled people to tell them what "the man" said, so that the people can decide whether they are satisfied or not and what to do about it.

The time for pussyfooting is long gone. If someone or other fears that some politician might be "embarrassed" by being confronted by such a delegation, or is concerned lest such action seem too bold, well, let that timid soul just step aside, for there are many in our ranks who will readily go in to "talk turkey" with any or all of the top men in government. We must get it into our heads and into every leader's head that we are not asking "favors" of the Big White Folks when, for example, we insist that the full power of the Executive be used to protect the right of Negroes to register and vote in the South. And when we really turn out for such a demand the answer can only be yes.

The *power of organization*, through which the power of numbers is expressed, is another great strength of the Negro people. Few other areas of American life are as intensively organized as is the Negro community. Some people say that we have far too many organizations—too many different churches and denominations, too many fraternal societies, clubs and associations—but that is what we have and there is no use deploring it. What is important is to recognize a meaningful fact which is so often denied: Negroes can and do band together, and they have accomplished remarkable works through their collective efforts. "The trouble with our folks"—how often you have heard it (or perhaps said it yourself)—"is that we just won't get together"; but the plain truth is that we just about do more joining and affiliating than anybody else. "Our folks are just not ready to make financial sacrifices for a good cause," we hear, and yet we see that all over the country congregations of a few hundred poor people contribute and collect thousands of dollars year in and year out for the purposes that inspire them...

The central role that was played in Montgomery by the churches and their pastors highlights the fact that the Negro church, which has played such a notable part in our history, is still the strongest base of our power of organization. This is true not only because of the large numbers who comprise the congregations, but because our churches are, in the main, independent Negro organizations. The churches and other groups of similar independent character—fraternal orders, women's clubs—and so forth, will increasingly take the lead because they are closer to the Negro rank-and-file, more responsive to their needs, and less subject to control by forces outside the Negro community...

It must be seen, too, that in relation to our general struggle for civil rights the Negro trade unionists occupy a key position. They comprise a large part of the membership of our community organizations and at the same time they are the largest section of our people belonging to interracial organizations. Hence, the Negro trade union members are a strategic link, a living connection with the great masses of the common people of America who are our natural allies in the struggle for democracy and whose active support must be won for our side in this critical hour...

To all groups in Negro life, I would say that the key to set into motion our power of organization is the concept of *coordinated action*, the bringing together of the many organizations which exist in order to plan and to carry out the common struggle. We know full well that it is not easy to do this. We are divided in many ways—in politics, in religious affiliations, in economic and social classes—and in addition to these group rivalries, there are the obstacles of the personal ambitions and jealousies of various leaders. But as I move among our people these days, from New York to California, I sense a growing impatience with petty ways of thinking and doing things. I see a rising resentment against control of our affairs by white people, regardless of whether that domination is expressed by the blunt orders of political bosses or more discreetly by the "advice" of white liberals which must be heeded or else. There is a rapidly growing awareness that despite all of our differences it is necessary that we become unified, and I think that the force of that idea will overcome all barriers. Coordinated action will not, of course, come all at once: it will develop in the grass-roots and spread from community to community. And the building of that unity is a task which each of us can undertake wherever we are...

I advocate a unity based upon our common viewpoint as Negroes, a nonpartisan unity, a unity in which we subordinate all that divides us, a unity which excludes no one, a unity in which no faction or group is permitted to impose its particular outlook on others. A unified leadership of a unified movement means that people of *all* political views—conservatives, liberals, and radicals—must be represented therein. Let there be but one requirement made without exception: that Negro leadership, and every man and woman in that leadership, place the interests of our people, and the struggle for those interests, above all else.

Paul Robeson studying his music, 1958

There is a need— an urgent need—for a national conference of Negro leadership, not of a handful but a broad representative gathering of leadership from all parts of the country, from all walks of life, from every viewpoint, to work out a *common program of action* for Negro Americans in the crisis of our times. Such a program does not exist today and without it we are a ship without a rudder; we can only flounder around on a day-to-day basis, trying to meet developments with patchwork solutions. We must chart a course to be followed in the stormy days that are here and in the greater storms that are on the way, a course that heads full square for freedom.

The need for a *central fund*, not only for legal purposes but for all the purposes of Negro coordinated action, has been expressed in various editorials in the press and elsewhere; and the national conference I speak of could meet this need. A central fund would be a "community chest" to help our struggles everywhere. Nonpartisan and not controlled by any single organization, this fund would be a national institution of our whole people, and a well-organized campaign to build it would meet with a generous response from Negro America. And more: such a fund would undoubtedly receive a great deal of support from white people who sympathize with our struggle.

If we must think boldly in terms of the power of numbers, we must likewise think big in terms of organization. Our cause is the cause of all, and so our methods of reaching our goal must be such that all of our people can play a part. The full potential of the Negro people's power of organization must be achieved in every city and state throughout the land.

The power of spirit that our people have is intangible, but it is a great force that must be unleashed in the struggles of today. A spirit of steadfast determination, exaltation in the face of trials—it is the very soul of our people that has been formed through all the long and weary years of our march toward free-

At children's summer camp, Crimea, USSR, 1958

dom. It is the deathless spirit of the great ones who have led our people in the past—Douglass, Tubman and all the others—and of the millions who kept "a-inching along." That spirit lives in our people's songs—in the sublime grandeur of "Deep River," in the driving power of "Jacob's Ladder," in the militancy of "Joshua Fit the Battle of Jericho," and in the poignant beauty of all our spirituals.

It lives in every Negro mother who wants her child "to grow up and be somebody," as it lives in our common people everywhere who daily meet insult and outrage with quiet courage and optimism. It is that spirit which gives that "something extra" to our athletes, to our artists, to all who meet the challenge of public performance. It is the spirit of little James Gordon of Clay, Kentucky, who, when asked by a reporter why he wanted to go to school with white children, replied: "Why shouldn't I?," and it is the spirit of all the other little ones in the South who have walked like mighty heroes through menacing mobs to go to school. It is the spirit of the elderly woman of Montgomery who explained her part in the bus boycott by saying: "When I rode in the Jim Crow buses my body was riding but my soul was walking, but now when my body is walking my soul is riding!"

Yes, that power of the spirit is the pride and glory of my people, and there is no human quality in all of America that can surpass it. It is a force only for good: there is no hatefulness about it. It exalts the finest things of life—justice and equality, human dignity and fulfillment. It is of the earth, deeply rooted, and it reaches up to the highest skies and mankind's noblest aspirations. It is time for this spirit to be evoked and exemplified in all we do, for it is a force mightier than all our enemies and will triumph over all their evil ways.

For Negro action to be decisive—given the favorable opportunity which I have outlined in the previous chapter and the sources of strength indicated above—still another factor is needed: *effective Negro leadership.*

The term "leadership" has been used to express many different concepts, and many of these meanings have nothing to do with what I am concerned with here. Individuals attain prominence for a wide variety of reasons, and often people who have climbed up higher on the ladder are called leaders though they make it plain that their sole interest is personal advancement, and the more elevated they are above all other Negroes the better they like it. Then, too, it has been traditional for the dominant group of whites, in local communities and on a national scale as well, to designate certain individuals as "Negro leaders," regardless of how the Negro people feel about it; and the idea is that Negro leadership is something that white folks can bestow as a favor or take away as punishment...

The primary quality that Negro leadership must possess, as I see it, is a *single-minded dedication to their people's welfare.* Any individual Negro, like any other person, may have many varied interests in life, but for the true leader all else must be subordinated to the interests of those whom he is leading. If today it can be said that the Negro people of the United States are lagging behind the progress being made by colored peoples in other lands, one basic cause for it has been that all too often Negro leadership here has lacked the selfless passion for their people's welfare that has characterized the leaders of the colonial liberation movements. Among us there is a general recognition—and a grudging acceptance—of the fact that some of our leaders are not only unwilling to make sacrifices but they must see some gain for themselves in whatever they do. A few crumbs for a few is too often hailed as "progress for the race." To live in freedom one must be prepared to die to achieve it, and while few if any of us are ever called upon to make that supreme sacrifice, no one can ignore the fact that in a difficult struggle those who are in the forefront may suffer cruel blows. He who is not prepared to face the trials of battle will never lead to a triumph. This spirit of dedication, as I have indicated, is abundantly present in the ranks of our people but progress will be slow until it is much more manifest in the character of leadership.

Dedication to the Negro people's welfare is one side of a coin: the other side is *independence.* Effective Negro leadership must rely upon and be responsive to no other control than the will of their people. We have allies—important allies—among our white fellow-citizens, and we must ever seek to draw them closer to us and to gain many more. But the Negro people's movement must be led by Negroes, not only in terms of title and position but in reality. Good advice is good no matter what the source and help is needed and appreciated from wherever it comes, but Negro action cannot be decisive if the advisers and helpers hold the guiding reins. For no matter how well-meaning other groups may be, the fact is our interests are secondary at best with them.

Today, such outside controls are a factor in reducing the independence and effectiveness of Negro leadership. I do not have in mind the dwindling group of Uncle Toms who shamelessly serve even an Eastland; happily, they are no longer of much significance. I have in mind, rather, those practices of Negro leadership that are based upon the idea that it is white power rather than Negro power that must be relied upon. This concept has been traditional since Booker T. Washington, and it has been adhered to by many who otherwise reject all notions of white supremacy. Even Marcus Garvey, who rose to leadership of a nationalist mass movement in the 1920s and who urged that the Negro peoples of the world "go forward to the point of destiny as laid out by themselves," believed that white power was decisive...

In Booker Washington's day it was the ruling white man of the South whose sympathy was considered indispensable; today it is the liberal section of the dominant group in the North whose goodwill is said to be the hope for Negro progress. It is clear that many Negro leaders act or desist from acting because they base themselves on this idea. Rejecting the concept that "white is right" they embrace its essence by conceding that "might is right." To the extent that this idea is prevalent in its midst, Negro leadership lacks the quality of independence without which it cannot be effective.

Dedication and independence—these are the urgent needs. Other qualities of leadership exist in abundance: we have many highly trained men and women, experienced in law, in politics, in civic affairs; we have spokesmen of great eloquence, talented organizers, skilled negotiators. If I have stressed those qualities which are most needed on the national level, it is not from any lack of appreciation for much that is admirable. On the local level, especially, there are many examples of dedicated and independent leadership. Indeed, the effective use of Negro power—of numbers, of organization, of spirit—in Montgomery was the result of Negro leadership of the highest caliber. And the whole nation has witnessed the heroic dedication of many other leaders in the South, who, at the risk of their lives and all they hold dear, are leading their people's struggles. There are many from our ranks who ought to be elevated to national leadership because by their deeds they have fully demonstrated their right to be there.

We should broaden our concept of leadership and see to it that all sections of Negro life are represented on the highest levels. There must be room at the top for people from down below. I'm talking about the majority of our folks who work in factory and field: they bring with them that down-to-earth view which is the highest vision, and they can hammer and plow in more ways than one. Yes, we need more of them in the leadership, and we need them in a hurry.

We need more of our women in the higher ranks, too, and who should know better than the children of Harriet Tubman, Sojourner Truth and Mary Church Terrell that our womenfolk have often led the way. Negro womanhood today is giving us many inspiring examples of steadfast devotion, cool courage under fire, and brilliant generalship in our people's struggles; and here is a major source for new strength and militancy in Negro leadership on every level.

But if there are those who ought to be raised to the top, there are some others already there who should be retired. I have noted, in another connection, that the Negro people are patient and long-suffering—sometimes to a fault. The fault is often expressed by permitting unworthy leaders to get away with almost anything. It is as if once a man rises to leadership, his responsibility to his people is no longer binding upon him.

But, in these critical days, we ought to become a little less tolerant, a little more demanding that all Negro leaders "do right." I have in mind, for example, the case of an important Negro leader in a large Northern city, who, at the time when mobs were barring the Negro children from high school in Little Rock and beating up Negro newspapermen, got up before his people and said: "We cannot meet this crisis by force against force. Under no circumstances can Federal troops be used. This would be a confession of our moral decadence, it would precipitate a second Civil War—it would open the stopper and send democracy down the drain for at least our generation and maybe forever." These words, so utterly devoid of any concern for his people and lacking all regard for the truth, were hardly spoken before the President sent in Federal troops! No civil war was started, democracy got a new lease on life, the mobs were dispersed, the Negro children were escorted to school, and for the first time since 1876 the lawful force of the Federal government was called out against the lawless force of White Supremacy in the South.

When, as in this case, a Negro leader vigorously opposes that which he should be fighting for and makes it clear that some other folks' interests are of more concern to him than his own people's—well, the so-called "politically wise" may say: "Oh, that's just politics—forget it." But the so-called "politically dumb" just can't see it that way. How can we be led by people who are not going our way?

Robeson with children in Budapest, Hungary, 1958

There are others, honest men beyond all doubt and sincerely concerned with their people's welfare, who seem to feel that it is the duty of a leader to discourage Negro mass action. They think that best results can be achieved by the quiet negotiations they carry on. And so when something happens that arouses the masses of people, and when the people gather in righteous anger to demand that militant actions be started, such men believe it their duty to cool things off.

We saw this happen not long ago when from coast to coast there was a great upsurge of the people caused by the brutal lynching of young Emmett Till. At one of the mass protest meetings that was held, I heard one of our most important leaders address the gathering in words to this effect: "You are angry today, but you are not going to do anything about it. I know that you won't do anything. You clamor for a march on Mississippi but none of you will go. So let's stop talking about marching. Just pay a dollar to our organization and leave the rest to your leaders. If you want to do something yourself, let each of you go to your district Democratic leader and talk to him about it."

Well, what would a congregation think of their pastor if the best he could do was to tell them: "You are all a bunch of sinners, and nothing can make you do right. There is no good in you and I know it. So, brothers and sisters, just put your contributions on the collection plate, go home and leave your salvation to me."

No, a leader should encourage, not discourage; he should rally the people, not disperse them. A wet blanket can never be the banner of freedom.

Of course there must be negotiations made in behalf of our rights, but unless the negotiators are backed by an aroused and militant people, their earnest pleas will be of little avail. For Negro action to be effective—to be decisive, as I think it can be—it must be *mass* action. The power of the ballot can be useful only if the masses of voters are united on a common program; obviously, if half the Negro people vote one way and the other half the opposite way, not much can be achieved. The individual votes are cast and counted, but the group power is cast away and discounted.

Mass action—in political life and elsewhere—is Negro power in motion; and it is the way to win.

An urgent task which faces us today is an all-out struggle to defeat the efforts of the White Supremacists to suppress the N.A.A.C.P. in the South. As in South Africa, where the notorious "Suppression of Communism Act" is used to attack the liberation movement, the enemies of Negro freedom in our country have accused the N.A.A.C.P. of being a "subversive conspiracy" and the organization has been outlawed in Louisiana, Texas and Alabama, and legally restricted in Georgia, Virginia, South Carolina and Mississippi. City ordinances, as in Little Rock, are also used for this purpose...

Throughout the South—in Little Rock, in Montgomery and elsewhere — the state and local leaders of the N.A.A.C.P. have set a heroic and inspiring example for Negro leadership everywhere. All of us—the Negro people of the entire country—must rally now to sustain and defend them.

In presenting these ideas on the power of Negro action, the sources of that power, and the character of leadership necessary to direct that power most effectively, I offer them for consideration and debate at this time when the challenge of events calls for clarity of vision and unity of action. No one, obviously, has all the answers, and the charting of our course must be done collectively. There must be a spirit of give and take, and clashing viewpoints must find a common ground. Partisan interests must be subordinated to Negro interests by each of us. Somehow we must find the way to set aside all that divides us and come together, Negroes all. Our unity will strengthen our friends and win many more to our side; and our unity will weaken our foes who already can see the handwriting on the wall.

To be free—to walk the good American earth as equal citizens, to live without fear, to enjoy the fruits of our toil, to give our children every opportunity in life— that dream which we have held so long in our hearts is today the destiny that we hold in our hands.

Rehearsing with Earl Robinson, 1960

Paul Robeson
Bearer of a Culture

A Retrospective and Interpretive Centennial Exhibition (1898-1998)

OBJECT LIST

I. ENTRANCE

R001. Yousuf Karsh portrait, 1940
Photograph
Courtesy of Paul Robeson, Jr.

R002. Original bronze head, by
Antonio Salemme, 1926
Courtesy of Paul Robeson, Jr.

Gallery I: Ascent To Manhood (1898-1929)

R003. Robeson's father, William
Drew Robeson, c. 1910
Photograph (blowup)
Courtesy of Paul Robeson, Jr.

R004. Robeson's mother, Louisa
Bustill Robeson, as a young woman,
c. 1885
Photograph
Courtesy of Paul Robeson, Jr.

R005. Robeson's father, William
Drew Robeson, c. 1885
Photograph
Courtesy of Paul Robeson, Jr.

R006. Portrait of Paul Robeson by
unidentified photographer, 1921
Photograph
Courtesy of Paul Robeson, Jr.

R007. Robeson as a Westfield Junior
High School student, age 12, with the
Westfield High School baseball team,
1910

Photograph
Courtesy of Paul Robeson, Jr.

R008. Robeson on the Somerville
High School football team, 1913
Photograph
Courtesy of Paul Robeson, Jr.

R009. Robeson on the Somerville
High School baseball team, 1914
Photograph
Courtesy of Paul Robeson, Jr.

R010. Robeson as football star at
Rutgers College, 1918
Photograph
Courtesy of Paul Robeson, Jr.

R011. Robeson in baseball catcher's uni-
form, conferring with coach and two
Rutgers College team members, 1919
Photograph
Courtesy of Rutgers University

R012. Robeson on the Rutgers
College baseball team, 1919
Photograph
Courtesy of Rutgers University

R013. Robeson on the Rutgers
College basketball team, 1917
Photograph
Courtesy of Rutgers University

R014. Robeson on the Rutgers
College track team, 1917
Photograph
Courtesy of Rutgers University

R015. Robeson in action during foot-
ball game between Rutgers and the
Naval Reserve, Ebbets Field, 1917
Photograph
Courtesy of Rutgers University

R016. Robeson on Rutgers College
football team, 1918
Photograph
Courtesy of Rutgers University

R017. Robeson of Rutgers: All-
America football player, 1917 and
1918 **Photograph** (blowup)
Courtesy of Rutgers University

R018. Robeson as member of
Rutgers Cap and Skull Society, 1918
Photograph
Courtesy of Rutgers University

R019. Robeson on Rutgers College
debating team, 1918
Photograph
Courtesy of Rutgers University

R020. Robeson as a junior at Rutgers
College, 1918
Photograph
Courtesy of Paul Robeson, Jr.

R021. Three snapshsots of Robeson
with friends, Rutgers College, c. 1917
Courtesy of Paul Robeson, Jr.

R022. Portrait of Paul Robeson,
1925, by unidentified photographer
Photograph

Courtesy of Paul Robeson, Jr.

CONTENTS OF CASE #1

R023. [c1] Marriage announcement and certificate, Paul Robeson and Eslanda Cardozo Goode, 1921
Courtesy of Paul Robeson, Jr.

R024 [c1] Robeson's law degree, Columbia University, 1923
Courtesy of Paul Robeson, Jr.

R025. [c1] Robeson's Phi Beta Kappa Key with charms, Rutgers College, 1918
Courtesy of Paul Robeson, Jr.

R026. [c1] Robeson's basketball charm, Rutgers College, 1918
Courtesy of Paul Robeson, Jr.

R027. [c1] Robeson's Rutgers College Diploma, 1919
Courtesy of Paul Robeson, Jr.

R028. [c1] Portrait of Robeson's wife, Eslanda Cardozo Goode Robeson, 1919
Courtesy of Paul Robeson, Jr.

R029. [c1] Two 1928 photographs: Mrs. Eslanda Cardozo Goode (Eslanda Robeson's mother) with Paul Robeson, Jr.; and Eslanda Robeson with Paul Robeson, Jr.
Courtesy of Gregory R. Smith

✳

R030. Portrait of Paul Robeson by Raphael, London, 1925
Photograph
Courtesy of Paul Robeson, Jr.

R031. Portrait of Eslanda Cardozo Goode Robeson by Sasha, London, 1925
Photograph Courtesy of Paul Robeson, Jr.

R032. Portrait of Paul and Eslanda Robeson, 1930
Photograph

Courtesy of Paul Robeson, Jr.

R033. Paul and Eslanda Robeson at Oak Bluffs, Martha's Vineyard, 1927 Three snapshots
Courtesy of Paul Robeson, Jr.

R034. Robeson with "Harmony Kings" trio, Plantation Club, New York, 1924
Photograph
Courtesy of Paul Robeson, Jr.

R035. Robeson in the Provincetown Playhouse production of *The Emperor Jones*, 1924
Photograph
Courtesy New York Public Library, Lincoln Center Library for the Performing Arts

R036. Film still from *Body and Soul*, 1924
Photograph
Courtesy of George Eastman House

R037. Robeson singing on stage in the 1932 production of the musical *Show Boat* at New York's Casino Theater
Photograph by Carl Van Vechten
Courtesy of the Carl Van Vechten Estate

R038. Cast on stage, *Show Boat*, London, 1928
Photograph
Courtesy of Paul Robeson, Jr.

R039. Cast on stage, *Show Boat*, London, 1928
Photograph
Courtesy of Paul Robeson, Jr.

R040. Robeson as Joe, *Show Boat*, London, 1928
Photograph
Courtesy of Paul Robeson, Jr.

CONTENTS OF CASE #2

R041. [c2] Play script from *Taboo*,

1922-1923
Courtesy of Paul Robeson, Jr.

R042. [c2] Robeson in *Voodoo (Taboo)*, 1922
Photograph
Courtesy of Paul Robeson, Jr.

R043. [c2] *The Complete Works of Eugene O'Neill, Volume 2*. New York: Boni and Liveright, 1924, with inscription from Eugene O'Neill to Paul Robeson
Courtesy of Paul Robeson, Jr.

R044. [c2] Eugene O'Neill (third from left) with Paul Robeson, Eslanda Robeson and others, c. 1924
Photograph
Courtesy of Paul Robeson, Jr.

R045. [c2] Play script from Eugene O'Neill's *The Emperor Jones*, 1924
Courtesy of Paul Robeson, Jr.

R046. [c2] Play script from Eugene O'Neill's *All God's Chillun Got Wings*, 1924
Courtesy of Paul Robeson, Jr.

R047. [c2] Letter from Aldous Huxley to Robeson with tribute poem, July 5, 1930
Courtesy of Paul Robeson, Jr.

R048. [c2] Program for the play *Black Boy*, 1926
Courtesy of Paul Robeson, Jr.

R049. [c2] Program from the play, *The Emperor Jones*, Provincetown Playhouse, 1924
Courtesy of Paul Robeson, Jr.

R050. [c2] Eslanda Robeson's 1924 diary, open to page describing premier of the play, *The Emperor Jones*
Courtesy of Paul Robeson, Jr.
R051. [c2] Letter from Eugene O'Neill to Eslanda Robeson,

April 10, 1930
Courtesy of Paul Robeson, Jr.

✳

R052. Paul Robeson with portable Victrola, London, 1933
Photograph
Courtesy of Paul Robeson, Jr.

R053. "His Master's Voice Records" Robeson Advertisement, London, 1928
Photograph
Courtesy of Paul Robeson, Jr.

R054. Portrait of Robeson by Sasha, London, 1925
Photograph
Courtesy of Paul Robeson, Jr.

R055A. Paul Robeson in performance at Royal Albert Hall, London, 1929
Photograph (blowup)
Courtesy of Paul Robeson, Jr.

R055B. Facsimile of New York newspaper reviews of Robeson, 1926
Photograph
Courtesy of Paul Robeson, Jr.

R056. Robeson recital announcement, Carnegie Hall, November 10, 1929
Photograph
Courtesy of Paul Robeson, Jr.

R057. Lawrence H. Brown musician, arranger and Robeson's acccompanist, at the piano, c. 1930
Photograph
Courtesy New York Public Library, Schomburg Center for Research in Black Culture

R058. Portrait of Robeson as Jim Harris in the 1933 London production of *All God's Chillun Got Wings*
Photograph by Helen MacGregor
Courtesy of Paul Robeson, Jr.
CONTENTS OF CASE #3

R059. [c3] Sheet music for *Ol' Man River*, from *Show Boat*, with original lyrics, 1927 (top)
Courtesy of Paul Robeson, Jr.

R060. [c3] Sheet music for *Ol' Man River*, from *Show Boat*, with altered lyrics, 1928 (bottom)
Courtesy of Paul Robeson, Jr.

R061. [c3] Robeson's pad of personal notes, 1929
Courtesy of Paul Robeson, Jr.

R062. [c3] Eslanda Robeson's 1926 diary, describing social events
Courtesy of Paul Robeson, Jr.

R063.[c3] Play script, *Show Boat*, 1928
Courtesy of Paul Robeson, Jr.

R064. [c3] Two Robeson Victor 78 rpm recordings, c. 1929, *Ol' Man River and Spiritual Medley*
Courtesy of Paul Robeson, Jr.

R065. [c3] Program from Drury Lane Theatre, *Show Boat*, 1928
Courtesy of Paul Robeson, Jr.

R066. [c3] Program from benefit recital at Harlem Museum of African Art, April 20, 1927
Courtesy of Paul Robeson, Jr.

R067. [c3] Program from recital at Greenwich Village Theater (Benefit concert for the Columbus Day Hill Nursery) March 15, 1925
Courtesy of Paul Robeson, Jr.

GALLERY II: ON TOP OF THE WORLD (1930-1947)

R068. Robeson in *Othello*, 1930
Photograph
Courtesy of Paul Robeson, Jr.

R069. Robeson with Peggy Ashcroft in *Othello*, 1930

Photograph
Courtesy of Paul Robeson, Jr.

R070. Filming *Borderline*, 1930. Paul and Eslanda Robeson with director Kenneth McPherson on location in Switzerland
Photograph
Courtesy of Paul Robeson, Jr.

R071. Robeson with Dudley Digges in a scene from the film version of *The Emperor Jones*, 1933
Photograph
Courtesy of Paul Robeson, Jr.

R072. Robeson in two stills from film, *The Emperor Jones*, 1933
Photographs
Courtesy of Paul Robeson, Jr.

R073. Portrait of Paul Robeson as *Emperor Jones* by Edward Steichen, 1933
Photograph
Courtesy of George Eastman House

R074. Portrait of Paul Robeson as *Emperor Jones* by Edward Steichen, 1933
Photograph
Courtesy of George Eastman House

R075. Facsimile poster for the film, *Show Boat*
Courtesy of Paul Robeson, Jr.

R076. Robeson on the set of the film, *Show Boat*, 1936
Photograph
Courtesy of Paul Robeson, Jr.

R077. London premiere of the film, *Song of Freedom*, 1936
Photograph
Courtesy of Paul Robeson, Jr.

R078. Robeson in still from *Jericho*, 1937
Photograph
Courtesy of Paul Robeson, Jr.

R079. Robeson in still from *King Solomon's Mines*, 1937
Photograph
Courtesy of Paul Robeson, Jr.

R080. Robeson in still from *Sanders of the River*, 1935
Photograph
Courtesy of Paul Robeson, Jr.

R081. Robeson in still from *Big Fella*, 1937
Photograph
Courtesy of Paul Robeson, Jr.

R082. Facsimile poster for *Big Fella*, 1937
Courtesy of Paul Robeson, Jr.

R083. Robeson in still from *Proud Valley*, 1939
Photograph
Courtesy of Paul Robeson, Jr.

R084. Robeson with Budd Schulberg, Ethel Waters, Clarence Muse and others in cast of the film, *Tales of Manhattan*, 1942
Photograph
Courtesy of Paul Robeson, Jr.

R085. Robeson singing to soldiers of the International Brigade in Republican Spain during the Spanish Civil War, 1938
Photograph by Eslanda Robeson
Courtesy of Paul Robeson, Jr.

R086. Robeson with Paul, Jr., Plymouth, England, 1936
Photograph
Courtesy of Bettmann Archives

R087. Robeson with Paul Jr., Kislovodsk, USSR, 1937
Photograph by Eslanda Robeson
Courtesy of Paul Robeson, Jr.

R088. Robeson on the cover of *Weekly Illustrated*, London, February 8, 1936

Courtesy of Paul Robeson, Jr.

R089. Robeson with Sergei Eisenstein on Robeson's arrival in Moscow, 1934
Photograph
Courtesy of Paul Robeson, Jr.

R090. Robeson in concert, Tchaikovsky Hall, Moscow, USSR, 1936
Photograph
Courtesy of Paul Robeson, Jr.

R091. Robeson in premiere performance of *Ballad for Americans*, on CBS Radio, November 5, 1939
Photograph
Courtesy of Paul Robeson, Jr.

R092. Robeson in repeat CBS broadcast of *Ballad for Americans*, January 1, 1940
Photograph
Courtesy of Paul Robeson, Jr.

R093. Cover page of *Ballad for Americans* sheet music, 1939
Courtesy of Paul Robeson, Jr.

R094. Robeson singing *Ballad for Americans* with People's Chorus, conducted by Dean Dixon, early 1940s
Photograph
Courtesy of Paul Robeson, Jr.

R095. Four images of Paul Robeson with his family, Enfield, Connecticut, 1941
Photographs by Frank Bauman
Courtesy of Paul Robeson, Jr.

CONTENTS OF CASE #4

R096. [c4] *Borderline*, film premiere booklet, 1930
Courtesy of Paul Robeson, Jr.

R097. [c4] Music for the song, "*Water Boy*," with marginalia
Courtesy of Paul Robeson, Jr.

R098. [c4] Letter from George Gershwin to Paul Robeson, April 25, 1934
Courtesy of Paul Robeson, Jr.

R099. [c4] *Show Boat* film premiere booklet
Courtesy of Paul Robeson, Jr.

R100. [c4] Universal Pictures performance contract with Paul Robeson for his participation in the film *Show Boat*
Courtesy of Paul Robeson, Jr.

R101. [c4] Letter from the Old Vic Theatre Company to Paul Robeson, November 13, 1936
Courtesy of Paul Robeson, Jr.

R102. [c4] Letter from Oscar Hammerstein II to Paul Robeson, October 17, 1935
Courtesy of Paul Robeson, Jr.

R103. [c4] Eslanda Robeson's diary, January 27, 1938, describing trip to Spain
Courtesy of Paul Robeson, Jr.

R104. [c4] Eslanda Robeson's diary, March 5, 1934, describing trip to Soviet Union (printed date on diary is incorrect)
Courtesy of Paul Robeson, Jr.

CONTENTS OF CASE #5

R105. [c5] Robeson's special ink and brushes for writing Chinese characters
Courtesy of Paul Robeson, Jr.

R106. [c5] *Paul Robeson, Negro*, 1930, book by Eslanda Robeson
Courtesy of Paul Robeson, Jr.

R107. [c5] *African Journey*, 1945 book by Eslanda Robeson
Courtesy of Paul Robeson, Jr.

R108. [c5] Pictorial Chinese-Japanese characters, book
Courtesy of Paul Robeson, Jr.

R109. [c5] *Negro Americans, What Now?*, book by James Weldon Johnson
Courtesy of Paul Robeson, Jr.

R110. [c5] *The Phonetic and Tonal Character of Efik*, book
Courtesy of Paul Robeson, Jr.

R111. [c5] *The Negro in the American Theater*, book
Courtesy of Paul Robeson, Jr.

R112. [c5] *Who's Who in Colored America*, book
Courtesy of Paul Robeson, Jr.

R113. [c5] *George Washington Carver*, book
Courtesy of Paul Robeson, Jr.

R114. [c5] *The Negro in American Civilization*, book
Courtesy of Paul Robeson, Jr.

R115. [c5] *Toward Freedom, The Autobiography of Jawaharlal Nehru*, book
Courtesy of Paul Robeson, Jr.

R116. [c5] *Practical Handbook of the Polish Language*, book
Courtesy of Paul Robeson, Jr.

R117. [c5] *Russian Basics and Essential Reader*, book
Courtesy of Paul Robeson, Jr.

R118. [c5] *The Case of Joe Hill*, book
Courtesy of Paul Robeson, Jr.

R119. [c5] German Edition of Shakespeare's *Othello*, book
Courtesy of Paul Robeson, Jr.

R120. [c5] *Peekskill, USA*, book by

Howard Fast
Courtesy of Paul Robeson, Jr.

R121. [c5] Short Course in *Kiswahili*, book
Courtesy of Paul Robeson, Jr.

R122. [c5] *Basic English*, book
Courtesy of Paul Robeson, Jr.

R123. [c5] *Conversational Japanese*, book
Courtesy of Paul Robeson, Jr.

R124. [c5] *Hebrew Grammar*, book
Courtesy of Paul Robeson, Jr.

R125. [c5] *Japanese in Thirty Hours*, book
Courtesy of Paul Robeson, Jr.

R126. [c5] *Basic Spanish*, book
Courtesy of Paul Robeson, Jr.

R127. [c5] *Elementary Chinese*, book
Courtesy of Paul Robeson, Jr.

R128. [c5] *Colloquial Czech*, book
Courtesy of Paul Robeson, Jr.

R129. [c5] *The History of the Black Phalanx*, book
Courtesy of Paul Robeson, Jr.

✳

R130. Robeson with (from left) Cab Calloway, Richard Wright, William Wesley the first African-American Fire Chief, and unidentified friend at the opening of the play *Native Son*, 1941
Photograph
Courtesy of Paul Robeson, Jr.

R131. Robeson with members of the African-American press, 1949
Photograph
Courtesy of *People's Weekly World*

R132. Robeson with Mary Church Terrell, 1947
Photograph
Courtesy of New York Public Library, Schomburg Center for

Research in Black Culture
R133. Robeson with Eleanor Roosevelt and Helen Hayes at Salute to Negro Troops, 1942
Courtesy of New York Public Library, Schomburg Center for Research in Black Culture

R134. Paul Robeson with Lena Horne during War Bond campaign, 1942
Photograph
Courtesy of Paul Robeson, Jr.

R135. Robeson with Lawrence Brown, Joe Louis, Marian Anderson, Bill Robinson and others at Rally to Promote Better Race Relations, Detroit, 1943
Photograph
Courtesy of New York Public Library, Schomburg Center for Research in Black Culture

R136. Robeson with Chinese friends at Stars for China War Relief benefit, May 2, 1941
Photograph
Courtesy of Paul Robeson, Jr.

R137. Robeson in Stalingrad, USSR, 1949
Photograph
Courtesy of Paul Robeson, Jr.

R138. Radio broadcast with Raymond Massey, New York, 1943
Photograph
Courtesy of Paul Robeson, Jr.

R139. Robeson speaking at Civil Rights Rally, Madison Square Garden, 1947
Photograph
Courtesy of Paul Robeson, Jr.

R140. Robeson with Vice President Henry Wallace, Sidney Hillman, Rexford Tugwell and friend, 1944
Photograph
Courtesy of Bettmann Archives

R141. Robeson speaking in Cadillac Square, Detroit to 100,000 striking auto workers, 1941
Photograph
Courtesy of *People's Weekly World*

R142. Robeson speaking at Convention of Union of Mine, Mill, and Smelter Workers, 1946
Photograph
Courtesy of *People's Weekly World*

R143. Robeson on picket line with Earl Robinson and others in front of Ford's Theater, St. Louis, 1947
Photograph
Courtesy of New York Public Library, Schomburg Center for Research in Black Culture

R144. Robeson in anti-segregation demonstration, Washington, D.C., 1948
Photograph
Courtesy of People's Weekly World

R145. Robeson picketing in front of the White House in support of Fair Labor practices, 1949
Photograph
Courtesy of People's Weekly World

R146. Robeson at Lincoln Memorial, Washington, D.C., September 23, 1946 as Co-Chairman of National Crusade To End Lynching (Albert Einstein was the other Co-Chairman)
Photograph
Courtesy of Bettmann Archives

R147. Robeson with Albert Einstein, Henry Wallace and friend, during Wallace's campaign for U.S. President on the Progressive Party ticket
Photograph
Courtesy of Bettmann Archives

CONTENTS OF CASE #6

R148. [c6] Robeson in uniform as leader of USO tour, 1945

Photograph
Courtesy of Paul Robeson, Jr.

R149. [c6] The National Association for the Advancement of Colored People (NAACP) Spingarn Medal, 1945
Courtesy of Paul Robeson, Jr.

R150. [c6] Robeson's USO uniform buttons, 1945
Courtesy of Paul Robeson, Jr.

R151. [c6] Robeson's itinerary of appearances, 1940s
Courtesy of Paul Robeson, Jr.

R152. [c6] Robeson performing in Prague, Czechoslovakia, 1949
Photograph
Courtesy of Paul Robeson, Jr.

R153. [c6] Examples of Robeson's on stage performance aids (song lyrics used as palm cards), 1940s
Courtesy of Paul Robeson, Jr.

R154. [c6] Abraham Lincoln Award, presented to Paul Robeson by Abraham Lincoln High School Brooklyn, New York, "To Honor Distinguished Service" on behalf of the City of New York, 1943
Courtesy of Paul Robeson, Jr.

R155. [c6] *We Want Peace* petition, ("Open Letter to Paul Robeson" in support of his "Fight to Preserve Peace"), 1949
Courtesy of Paul Robeson, Jr.

R156. [c6] Telegram of support for Robeson from Jawaharlal Nehru, 1949
Courtesy of Paul Robeson, Jr.

R157. [c6] Printed invitation to the Robesons from Jawaharlal Nehru, 1949
Courtesy of Paul Robeson, Jr.

R158. [c6] A sampling of Robeson's

honorary labor union membership cards, 1940s
Courtesy of Paul Robeson, Jr.

R159. [c6] Inscribed ring given to Paul Robeson, made from the last German shell to fall on one of the main bastions in defense of Stalingrad during World War II
Courtesy of Paul Robeson, Jr.

R160. [c6] Letter from Jawaharlal Nehru to Eslanda Robeson, July 10, 1940
Courtesy of Paul Robeson, Jr.

CONTENTS OF CASE #7

R161. [c7] 78 rpm record album of Shakespeare's *Othello*, as performed on Broadway by Robeson and cast, 1943-1944 (recorded in 1946)
Courtesy of Paul Robeson, Jr.

R162. [c7] Robe worn by Paul Robeson in 1943-1944 Broadway production of Shakespeare's *Othello*
Courtesy of Paul Robeson, Jr.

R163. [c7] "Paul Robeson as Othello," Standing figure by Richmond Barthe, 1975 Bronze
Courtesy of Actors Equity, The Paul Robeson Awards Committee

✳

R164. Program for 1943-1944 Paul Robeson Broadway production of Shakespeare's *Othello*
Courtesy of Paul Robeson, Jr.

R165. Robeson with Uta Hagen as Desdemona in 1943-1944 production of Shakespeare's *Othello*
Photograph
Courtesy of Paul Robeson, Jr.

R166. Paul Robeson as Othello, 1943-1944 Broadway production
Photograph (blowup)
Courtesy of New York Public Library, Lincoln Center Library for the

Performing Arts

R167. Bust of Paul Robeson as Othello, by Richmond Barthe, 1975, Bronze
Courtesy of Actors Equity, The Paul Robeson Awards Committee

R168. Robeson with Carl Van Vechten, 1946
Photograph
Courtesy of Time/Life Syndication

R169. Portrait of Paul Robeson by Gordon Parks, 1940
Photograph
Courtesy of Library of Congress

GALLERY III: IN SEARCH OF FREEDOM (1948-1976)

R170. Robeson at rally celebrating his return from European trip,
June 19, 1949
Photograph
Courtesy of Paul Robeson Foundation

R171. Robeson at the wedding of his son, Paul Jr. and Marilyn P. Greenberg, June 19, 1949
Photograph
Courtesy of *People's Weekly World*

R172. Robeson speaking at New York civil rights meeting, 1949
Photograph
Courtesy of Paul Robeson, Jr.

R173. Robeson singing at the Paris Peace Conference, April, 1949
Photograph
Courtesy of Time/Life Syndication

R174. Robeson with W.E.B. DuBois at the Paris Peace Conference, April 1949
Photograph
Courtesy of Bettmann Archives

R175. Eugene Bullard, World War I ace pilot, on the ground after being

beaten by police at the second Robeson Peekskill concert,
September 4, 1949
Photograph
Courtesy of the New York Public Library, Schomburg Center for Research in Black Culture

R176. Concert-goers being harassed at the first, aborted Robeson Peekskill concert, August 27, 1949
Photograph
Courtesy of Bettmann Archives

R177. Human wall of trade union guards protecting Robeson at the second Peekskill concert,
September 4, 1949
Photograph
Courtesy of the New York Public Library, Schomburg Center for Research in Black Culture

R178. Robeson on the platform at the second Peekskill concert, September 4, 1949. The men standing behind him are shielding him with their bodies from a possible sniper's bullet.
Photograph
Courtesy of the *People's Weekly World*

R179-182. Four views of the Peekskill aftermath, New York, 1949
Photographs
Courtesy of Bettmann Archives

R183. Robeson at the Canadian border at Blaine, Washington in 1952, where he was prevented by the US Immigration Service from crossing into Canada
Photograph
Courtesy of the New York Public Library, Schomburg Center for Research in Black Culture

R184. Paul and Eslanda Robeson, 1958
Photograph
Courtesy of Paul Robeson, Jr.

R185-194. [c8] *Here I Stand*, written in 1957 by Paul Robeson in collaboration with Lloyd L. Brown (published in 1958). Blowup of cover, US edition, and eight foreign editions in translation
Courtesy of Paul Robeson, Jr.

R195. [c8] U.S. edition of *Here I Stand* with marginalia in Russian by Paul Robeson
Courtesy of Paul Robeson, Jr.

R196. Robeson testifying before the House Committee on Un-American Activities, 1956
Photograph
Courtesy of Bettmann Archives

R197. Facsimile front page of newspaper *The Afro-American*, June 23, 1956, with coverage of
Robeson's appearance before the House Committee on Un-American Activities
Courtesy of Paul Robeson, Jr.

R198. Robeson on stage during 1949 European concert tour
Photograph
Courtesy of Paul Robeson, Jr.

R199. Robeson with Leontyne Price at joint concert, Dayton, Ohio, 1952
Photograph
Courtesy of Paul Robeson, Jr.
R200. Robeson singing outside a small rural church in Oregon, 1948
Photograph
Courtesy of New York Public Library, Schomburg Center for Research in Black Culture

R201. Robeson speaking at Paris Peace Conference, April, 1949
Photograph (blowup)
Courtesy of Time/Life Syndication

R202. Reverend Benjamin C. Robeson, Paul Robeson's older brother, 1950
Photograph
Courtesy of Paul Robeson, Jr.

R203. Family photograph at christening of David Paul Robeson, Paul Robeson's grandson, 1952. Standing with Paul Robeson: Rev. Benjamin C. Robeson and his wife, Frances; Paul, Jr. Seated: Lillie Albertson, David's godmother, holding David; Marilyn Robeson and Eslanda Robeson
Photograph by Austen Hansen
Courtesy of Paul Robeson, Jr.

R204. Paul Robeson, c. 1950
Photograph by unidentified photographer
Courtesy of Paul Robeson, Jr.

R205. Robeson speaking in Moscow, USSR at the sesquicentennial of the birth of Alexander Pushkin, 1949
Photograph
Courtesy of Paul Robeson, Jr.

R206. Robeson in St. Paul's Cathedral, London, 1958
Photograph
Courtesy of Paul Robeson, Jr.

CONTENTS OF CASE #9

R207. [c9] Three passports issued to Paul Robeson, 1941; 1958; 1962
Courtesy of Paul Robeson, Jr.

R208. [c9] Robeson's application for a passport
Courtesy of Paul Robeson, Jr.

R209. [c9] Robeson with restored passport, 1958
Photograph
Courtesy of *People's Weekly World*

R210. [c9] "We Charge Genocide"

typescript (petition presented to the United Nations by Robeson on behalf of the Civil Rights Congress), 1951
Courtesy of Paul Robeson, Jr.

R211. [c9] Robeson handwritten speech "I've Been Busy," transcribed by Eslanda Robeson, c. 1958
Courtesy of Paul Robeson, Jr.

R212. [c9] Program of Robeson's appearance in St. Paul's Cathedral, London, 1958
Courtesy of Paul Robeson, Jr.

R213. [c9] US Congress subpoena of Robeson to appear before House Committee on Un-American Activities, May 29, 1956
Courtesy of Paul Robeson, Jr.

R214. [c9] United States Information Agency letter from Edward R. Murrow regarding Robeson, January 23, 1963
Courtesy of Paul Robeson, Jr.

R215. [c9] Memorandum from FBI Director J. Edgar Hoover to Lawrence Smith regarding Paul Robeson, January 12, 1943
Courtesy of Paul Robeson, Jr.

R216. [c9] FBI General Security Memorandum on Robeson, January 29, 1947
Courtesy of Paul Robeson, Jr.

R217. [c9] Letter from George Bernard Shaw to Robeson, June 13, 1950
Courtesy of Paul Robeson, Jr.

R218. Cover of the Soviet satirical magazine, *Crocodile*, 1956
Courtesy of Paul Robeson, Jr.

R219. Robeson at funeral service for Lorraine Hansberry, January 16, 1965

Photograph
Courtesy of Bettmann Archives

R220. Robeson at 77th birthday party at his sister Marian's house in Philadelphia, April 9, 1975
Color Photograph
Courtesy of Paul Robeson, Jr.

R221. Robeson performance poster, London, 1960
Courtesy of Paul Robeson, Jr.

R222. Robeson family portrait, New York, 1957. Standing, from left: Marilyn Robeson; Eslanda Robeson, Paul Robeson, Jr. Seated, from left: Susan Robeson, Paul Robeson, David Paul Robeson
Photograph
Courtesy of Paul Robeson, Jr.

R223. Robeson at *Freedomways* Salute to Paul Robeson, Americana Hotel, New York, April 22, 1965
Photograph by Beauford Smith
Courtesy of Paul Robeson, Jr.

CONTENTS OF CASE #10

R224. [c10] Selection of three letters written by Paul Robeson to Bob and Clara Rockmore, 1960, 1961
Courtesy of Paul Robeson, Jr.

CONTENTS OF CASE #11

R225. [c11] 1972 Citation for Paul Robeson's induction into the National Theater Hall of Fame as a charter member
Courtesy of Paul Robeson, Jr.

R226. [c11] Hollywood Walk of Fame "Star'" awarded posthumously to Paul Robeson
Courtesy of Paul Robeson, Jr.

R227. [c11] Stalin Peace Prize, 1952
Courtesy of Paul Robeson, Jr.

R228. [c11] Program for Paul Robeson's funeral service, January 27, 1976
Courtesy of Paul Robeson, Jr.

R229. [c11] National Academy of Recording Arts and Sciences, Lifetime Achievement "Grammy" Award, presented to Paul Robeson posthumously February 24, 1998
Courtesy of Paul Robeson, Jr.

R230. [c11] Miner's lamp, presented to Paul Robeson by South Wales Area National Union of Mine Workers
Courtesy of Paul Robeson, Jr.

R231. [c11] Medal for Achievement in Art, presented to Paul Robeson by the

German Democratic Republic, 1960
Courtesy of Paul Robeson, Jr.

R232. [c11] Ceremonial axe sent to Paul Robeson by an Ovibundu chief (southern Angola) after hearing Robeson sing *Water Boy* on a portable gramophone brought by an anthropological expedition in 1946
Courtesy of Paul Robeson, Jr.

R233. [c11] Black Athletes' Hall of Fame Medal, presented posthumously to Paul Robeson
Courtesy of Paul Robeson, Jr.

R234. [c11] United Nations Medal for Distinguished Service in the

Struggle against Apartheid, presented posthumously to Paul Robeson
Courtesy of Paul Robeson, Jr.

✳

R235. David Paul Robeson
Color Photograph
Courtesy of Paul Robeson, Jr.

R236. Jacob Epstein, head of Paul Robeson, 1927 Bronze
Courtesy of a private collector.

R237. Charles White portrait of Paul Robeson, 1973 oil wash
Courtesy of The Paul Robeson Foundation

Exhibition Credits

Co-Curators:	Julia Hotton, Paul Robeson Foundation Jack Rutland, The New-York Historical Society
Designer:	J.R. Sanders, Sanders Design Works, Inc.
Writer:	Marilyn Robeson
Audio Visual Editor:	Jack Rutland
Consultant:	Paul Robeson, Jr.

———————

The Paul Robeson Foundation expresses their gratitude to the New-York Historical Society staff for their dedication in the development, production and outreach for this Exhibition.

———————

This Exhibition is sponsored by The Paul Robeson Foundation. Funders include the Vincent Astor Foundation, the Bildner Family Foundation, Ken Boxley, David Rockefeller and the Rockefeller Brothers Fund.

This Exhibition would not have been possible without the tireless and invaluable assistance of Paul Robeson, Jr. and Marilyn Robeson, who provided unlimited access to the remarkable Robeson Collections and who provided important guidance throughout this project.

A Paul Robeson Chronology 1898-1998

1898 April 9: Paul Leroy Robeson born in Princeton, New Jersey, son of a former slave.

1904 Mother dies in household fire. William Drew Robeson, a minister, raises his five children.

1915 Wins a competitive examination for a four-year scholarship to Rutgers; makes varsity football team despite racist hostility.

1918 Father dies at age 73. Chosen for the All-American football team and elected to Phi Beta Kappa.

1919 Graduates from Rutgers with highest honors, delivers valedictory address and moves to Harlem.

1920 Enters Columbia Law School. Plays professional football.

1921 Marries Eslanda Cardozo Goode, analytical chemist.

1922 Appears in Mary Hoyt Wiborg's play *Taboo* in New York and in English production called *Voodoo*, with Mrs. Patrick Campbell.

1923 Graduates from Columbia Law School. Supports himself singing at Plantation Club while seeking law work.

1924 Opens in Eugene O'Neill's *All God's Chillun Got Wings* to great success. Makes silent film *Body and Soul*, stars in O'Neill's *The Emperor Jones*.

1925 Sings the first performance of Negro spirituals on concert stage.

1927 Tours Europe with concerts of spirituals. Victor Records releases first album.

1928 Overnight sensation in London in *Show Boat* for "Ol' Man River," written for him by Kern and Hammerstein.

1930 Stars to great acclaim in *Othello* in London.

1933 Films *The Emperor Jones*. Plays a benefit for Jewish refugees from Nazism. Studies African languages.

1934 Visits Soviet Union for the first time. Impressed by Soviet opposition to racism. 1936 films in Hollywood and London: *Show Boat, The Song of Freedom, King Solomon's Mines*.

1937 Co-founder of Council of African Affairs, to aid national liberation in Africa. Goes to Spain. Sings at numerous concerts for Spanish Republican cause.

1939 Tours U.S., often encountering segregation; sings "Ballad for Americans."

1940 Opens in musical *John Henry* on Broadway.

1942 Speaks, sings and tours war plants for war effort and fight against fascism.

1943 Opens on Broadway in *Othello* to ten curtain calls. Placed by J. Edgar Hoover on Custodial Detention List as threat to security in case of national emergency.

1945 Awarded NAACP Springarn Medal.

1946 Speaks for African colonial liberation, joins worker picket lines, meets President Truman for Crusade Against Lynching.

1948 Campaigns for Henry Wallace, presidential candidate of Progressive Party. Before Senate committee, states that questions about party membership violate First Amendment.

1949 Rock-throwing mob stops outdoor concert at Peekskill, New York. One week later, successful concert for 25,000 is followed by mob attack on audience.

1950 Barred by NBC from Eleanor Roosevelt's TV program. Opposes U.S. role in Korean War. Passport revoked by State Department.

1951 Heads New York delegation of Civil Rights Congress, presenting petition to U.N. charging genocide against Negroes in the United States.

1952 Awarded Stalin Peace Prize in New York.

1955 Refuses to sign non-Communist oath for new passport.

1956 Tells House Un-American Activities Committee, "You are the Un-Americans."

1958 Gives first New York concert in ten years at sold-out Carnegie Hall, announcing victory in passport battle through worldwide campaign. Publishes autobiography *Here I Stand* to boycott from white media. Tours Europe and Soviet Union, falling ill in Moscow.

1959 Stars in *Othello* at 100th season of England's Stratford-upon-Avon, Memorial Theatre.

1963 Returns to U.S. after five year absence, and continues civil rights work.

1965 Retires to Philadelphia after Eslanda Robeson's death.

1972 Inducted as charter member into National Theater Hall of Fame.

1973 Salute to Paul Robeson on 75th birthday packs Carnegie Hall.

1976 Dies at age 77. Five thousand attend funeral at Mother AME Zion Church in Harlem.

1983 Awarded a star in Hollywood's Sidewalk of Stars.

1995 Inducted into National College Football Hall of Fame after 47 years of exclusion for political reasons.

1998 Awarded a Grammy Lifetime Achievement Award.

BOOKS

I. *HERE I STAND*, by Paul Robeson; Beacon Press, Boston, 1958.

Robeson Resource Guide

BOOKS

I. *HERE I STAND*, by Paul Robeson; Beacon Press, Boston, 1958.

II. *THE WHOLE WORLD IN HIS HANDS*, A Pictorial Biography of Paul Robeson, by Susan Robeson; Citadel Press, Secaucus, New Jersey. [To order a copy, call 1-800-447-2665.]

III. *PAUL ROBESON*, by Marie Seton; Dobson Books, United Kingdom.

IV. *PAUL ROBESON SPEAKS*, by Philip S. Foner; Citadel Press, Secaucus, New Jersey.

V. *PAUL ROBESON, THE GREAT FORERUNNER*, by the editors of *Freedomways*; Dodd, Meade & Company, New York.

VI. *PAUL ROBESON, SINGER AND ACTOR*, by Scott Ehrlich. *Black Americans of Achievement series*; Chelsea House Publishers, N.Y.

VII. *THE YOUNG PAUL ROBESON, "On My Journey Now"*, by Lloyd L. Brown; Westview Press, a Division of Harper Collins Publishers.

VIII. *PAUL ROBESON: THE LIFE AND TIMES OF A FREE BLACK MAN*, by Virginia Hamilton; Dell Publishing Co, Inc., 1974.

IX. *PAUL ROBESON: HIS CAREER IN THE THEATER, IN MOTION PICTURES, AND ON THE CONCERT STAGE*, Anatol I. Schlosser, Doctoral Dissertation, New York University, Tamiment Library. Copyright 1970.

X. *PAUL ROBESON*, by Eloise Greenfield, illustrated by George Ford; Thomas Y. Crowell Co., New York, 1975. (34 pp.; for young children.)

XI. *PEEKSKILL: USA*, by Howard Fast, Civil Rights Congress, 1951.

COMPACT DISCS

I. *THE ODYSSEY OF PAUL ROBESON*, Omega Classics, #OCD 3007. [27 West 72nd Street, NY 10023; (212) 769-3060.]

II. *PAUL ROBESON, The Power and the Glory*, Columbia Legacy, #47337 AAD.

III. *PAUL ROBESON, The Legendary Moscow Concert*, "Forbidden Treasures of the Empire" series; Fenix Entertainment, Burbank, California.

IV. *THE COLLECTOR'S PAUL ROBESON*, Monitor, #MCD-61580.

V. *PAUL ROBESON, A Lonesome Road*, Academy Sound and Vision, Ltd., #CD AJA5027.

VI. *SHAKESPEARE'S OTHELLO, WITH THE ORIGINAL BROADWAY 1943-1944 CAST*, [Originally Columbia CSL series (now Sony Classical)].

VII. *PAUL ROBESON Sings Ol' Man River*, EMI, #CDC-7 47839 2.

VIII. *PAUL ROBESON*, Pearl, #CD 9382.

IX. *PAUL ROBESON, Ol' Man River*, Conifer Records Ltd., #CDHD 183.

X. *PAUL ROBESON*, Flapper, #PAST CD 7009.

XI. *PAUL ROBESON AND ELIZABETH WELCH*, Conifer Records Ltd., #CMSCD 011.

XII. *PAUL ROBESON: Songs Of Free Men*, Sony Classical, Masterworks Heritage; #MHK63223.

XIII. *PAUL ROBESON: BALLAD FOR AMERICANS*, Welk Music Group, 1299 Ocean Avenue, Santa Monica, CA 90401; Tel. (310) 451-5727.

AUDIO CASSETTES

I. *THE ODYSSEY OF PAUL ROBESON*, Omega Classics, #OCD 3007. [27 West 72nd Street, NY 10023; (212) 769-3060.]

II. *PAUL ROBESON, The Power and the Glory*, Columbia Legacy, #47337 AAD.

III. *PAUL ROBESON, The Legendary Moscow Concert*, "Forbidden Treasures of the

Empire" series; Fenix Entertainment, Burbank, California.

IV. THE COLLECTOR'S PAUL ROBESON, Monitor, #MCD-61580.

V. *PAUL ROBESON, A Lonesome Road*, Academy Sound and Vision, Ltd., #CD AJA5027.

VI. *SHAKESPEARE'S OTHELLO, WITH THE ORIGINAL BROADWAY CAST 1943-1944.* [Columbia CSL series (now Sony Classical)].

VII. *TRIBUTE TO PAUL ROBESON, WBAI, PACIFICA RADIO, 1973 (2hrs 35 min)*, produced by Charles Hobson.

VIII. *PAUL ROBESON, The Great Forerunner*; two-hour radio program about Paul Robeson: panel discussion and archival tapes; part of "PASSING IT ON II, Voices From Black America's Past." [By Media Works, 1996; 7831 Woodmont Ave., Suite 320, Bethesda, Maryland 20814; Tel. (301) 570-6339.]

VIDEO CASSETTES

I. *PAUL ROBESON: Tribute to an Artist*, produced by Saul Turell, 1980, Janus Films, 1 Bridge Street, Irvington, NY 10533. (914) 591-5500.

II. *PAUL ROBESON*, BBC documentary, produced by Geoffrey Baines. [United Kingdom, 1981].

III. *SONGS OF FREEDOM*; Channel 4 TV United Kingdom documentary on Paul Robeson, 1985; produced by Mike Wallington and Howard Johnson.

IV. *PAUL ROBESON: The Tallest Tree in Our Forest*, WABC/TV, 1974; produced by Gil Noble, "Like It Is," 7 Lincoln Square, NY 10023.

V. *PAUL ROBESON: A Closer Look*, WABC/TV, 1979; produced by Gil Noble, "Like It Is," 7 Lincoln Square, NY 10023.

VI. *PAUL ROBESON, Man of Conscience*, WNET, New York City; 30-minute Janus Films documentary on Paul Robeson, plus 30-minute question period conducted by Paul Robeson, Jr. [February 24, 1986 at the American Museum of Natural History.]

VII. *A Profile of Paul Robeson*, by Tony Batten, 1971; WNET, Washington, D.C.

VIII. *TRIBUTE TO PAUL ROBESON*, WNET "New Jersey Speaks," 1973, produced by Betsy Pilat Marsten.

FEATURE FILMS

I. *Body and Soul*, by Oscar Michaux, 1924. [George Eastman House, Rochester N.Y.]

II. *Borderline*, by Kenneth McPherson, 1930. [George Eastman House, Rochester, N.Y.]

III. *The Emperor Jones*, 1933; Janus Films [(914) 591-5500].

IV. *Sanders of the River*; 1935, United Kingdom Film Archives.

V. *Show Boat*, Universal Pictures,1936.

VI. *Song of Freedom*, 1937, United Kingdom Film Archives.

VII. *King Solomon's Mines*, 1937, Janus Films.

VIII. *Big Fella*, London, 1938 [Estate of Raymond Rohauer].

IX. *Jericho (Dark Sands)*, London, 1938 [Estate of Raymond Rohauer].

X. *The Proud Valley*, 1940, Janus Films.

XI. *Tales of Manhattan*, 1942; United Kingdom Film Archives.

DOCUMENTARY FILMS

I. *My Song Goes Forth*, 1936; documentary about South Africa, narrated by Paul Robeson; United Kingdom Film Archives.

II. *Native Land*, by Leo Hurwitz; 1941 documentary about U.S. labor and civil rights, narrated by Paul Robeson; Estate of Leo Hurwitz.

III. Polish documentary: *Paul Robeson in Warsaw*, 1949; Film Polski and Janus Films.

IV. Soviet documentary: *Paul Robeson in the USSR*, 1959, by Vasili Katanian; Russian Documentary Film Archives.

V. East German documentary: *Paul Robeson Bei Uns*, 1961; Paul Robeson Archives, Berlin, Academy of the Arts.

VI. *A Profile of Paul Robeson*, by Tony Batten, 1971, WNET, Washington, D.C.

VII. *Paul Robeson: The Tallest Tree in Our Forest*, by Gil Noble, 1974; WABC/TV, 7 Lincoln Plaza, New York, NY 10023,

(212) 456-7777.

VIII. *Paul Robeson, a Closer Look*, by Gil Noble, 1979; WABC/TV, 7 Lincoln Plaza, New York, NY 10023, (212) 456-7777.

IX. *Paul Robeson, Tribute to an Artist*, by Saul Turell, 1980; Janus Films.

X. *Paul Robeson*, BBC documentary by Geoffrey Baines, 1981; BBC, London.

XI. *Songs of Freedom*, Channel 4 TV documentary on Paul Robeson by Mike Wallington and Howard Johnson; 1985, London.